Wordsworth and the Motions of the Mind

American University Studies

Series IV
English Language and Literature
Vol. 93

PETER LANG
New York • Bern • Frankfurt am Main • Paris

Gordon Kent Thomas

Wordsworth
and the Motions
of the Mind

72891

PETER LANG
New York • Bern • Frankfurt am Main • Paris

Library of Congress Cataloging-in-Publication Data

Thomas, Gordon Kent
   Wordsworth and the motions of the mind / Gordon
Kent Thomas.
     p. cm. — (American university studies. Series IV,
English language and literature ; vol. 93)
    Bibliography: p.
    Includes index.
    1. Wordsworth, William, 1770-1850—Criticism and
interpretation. 2. Wordsworth, William, 1770-1850—
Knowledge—Education. 3. Didactic poetry, English—
History and criticism. 4. Intellect in literature.
5. Education in literature. I. Title. II. Series.
PR5892.D52T47   1989   821′.7—dc19   89-2756
ISBN 0-8204-1012-8   CIP
ISSN 0741-0700

CIP-Titelaufnahme der Deutschen Bibliothek

Thomas, Gordon Kent:
Wordworth and the motions of the mind /
Gordon Kent Thomas. — New York; Bern;
Frankfurt am Main; Paris: Lang, 1989.
  (American University Studies: Ser. 4, English
  Language and Literature; Vol. 93)
  ISBN 0-8204-1012-8

NE: American University Studies / 04

Printed by Weihert-Druck GmbH, Darmstadt, West Germany

CONTENTS

Works by Wordsworth and his contemporaries frequently cited in the text are identified by the following abbreviations:

BL, ed. Shawcross   Coleridge, Samuel Taylor. *Biographia Literaria*. Ed. John Shawcross. 2 vols. Oxford: Clarendon, 1907.

BL, ed. Watson   _____. *Biographia Literaria*. Ed. George Watson. London: Dent, 1965.

BLJ   Byron, George Gordon (Lord). *Byron's Letters and Journals*. Ed. Leslie A. Marchand. 12 vols. London: John Murray, 1973–82.

DJ   _____. *Don Juan*. Ed. Jerome J. McGann. Oxford: Clarendon, 1986. Vol. 5 of *Lord Byron: The Complete Poetical Works*. 1980–. 5 vols. to date.

EY
MY   Wordsworth, William, and Dorothy Wordsworth.
LY   *The Letters of William and Dorothy Wordsworth*. Vol. 1, *The Early Years*. Ed. Chester L. Shaver. Cited as *EY*. Vols. 2 and 3, *The Middle Years*. Ed. Mary Moorman and Alan G. Hill. Cited as *MY*. Vols. 4–6 to date, *The Later Years*. Ed. Alan G. Hill. Cited as *LY*. Oxford: Clarendon, 1967–. 6 vols. to date.

Griggs   Coleridge, Samuel Taylor. *Collected Letters*. Ed. Earl Leslie Griggs. 6 vols. Oxford: Clarendon, 1956–71.

PW   Wordsworth, William. *The Poetical Works of William Wordsworth*. 1940–49. Ed. Ernest de Selincourt and Helen Darbishire. 5 vols. Oxford: Clarendon, 1952–59.

Prelude   _____. *The Prelude, 1799, 1805, 1850*. Ed. Jonathan Wordsworth, M. H. Abrams, and Stephen Gill. New York: Norton, 1979. Unless otherwise noted, the 1850 ed. is used.

Prose   _____. *The Prose Works of William Wordsworth*. Ed. W. J. B. Owen and Jane Worthington Smyser. 3 vols. Oxford: Clarendon, 1974.

ACKNOWLEDGMENTS

The Wordsworth Summer Conference at Dove Cottage, held each August in Grasmere, along with its February sister, the Wordsworth Winter School, is the most interesting, delightful, and valuable international gathering of scholars, students, and aficionados with a specific literary focus and locus that I have ever encountered. Many of the ideas and even a number of the phrases of this book had their first public presentation at sessions of that conference over the years since 1983. I am grateful to colleagues from many places who have gathered in Grasmere and who have listened to my lectures, responded to them, and helped in the refining of my ideas. I am particularly grateful to Richard and Sylvia Wordsworth, dear friends and superb organizers of the Wordsworth Conference, for repeated invitations to that best of Wordsworthian places and for their tireless skill and effort in making it what it is.

To Richard Wordsworth, who by his having accepted a visiting professorship at Brigham Young University became my close colleague and thereby laid himself open to such request, I am also indebted for his having read and offered helpful comments on the manuscript version of this book. He has shared that chore with others to whom I also express my deepest thanks: Norman Fruman of the University of Minnesota, Thomas McFarland of Princeton University, and Sue Weaver Schopf of the Humanities School of Continuing Education at Harvard—all of them true friends, colleagues, exemplars.

Early versions of portions of three chapters of this work have appeared in *The Wordsworth Circle*, as follows: part of chapter 3, under the title "Surprised by Joy: Wordsworth and the Princes of Serendip," in the Spring 1986 issue (17: 80–87); part of chapter 7, under the title " 'The Thorn' in the Flesh of English Romanticism," in the Autumn 1983 issue (14: 237–43); and a portion of chapter 8 entitled "A Guide to Wordsworth's Guides" in the Winter 1987 issue (18: 28–32). This is an appropriate spot not only to note that versions of these segments of this book have already appeared in print, but to express my thanks for a long and valued association with that fine journal and its excellent and helpful editor, Marilyn Gaull.

I am grateful to have been granted a fellowship, since the fall of 1986, with the David M. Kennedy Center for International Studies at Brigham Young University, under the direction of Professor Ray Hillam; the support and encouragement, the privacy and time which that fellowship has afforded me have been not merely welcome but crucial in the completion of this work.

Finally, I express my deep personal gratitude and admiration to Linda Hunter Adams, managing director of the Humanities Publications Center at Brigham Young University and her excellent staff, particularly Philip White, Scott Patrick, Tim Hiatt, and Bruce Pritchett, for their immensely helpful and professional work in readying the manuscript for publication.

CHAPTER ONE

The Motions of the Mind

"Didactic poetry is my abhorrence," wrote Percy Bysshe Shelley in his preface to *Prometheus Unbound*. Most modern readers, at least readers of some sophistication, probably share that attitude. But didacticism has not always been considered a poetic evil. Joseph Warton in his 1756 *Essay on the Writings and Genius of Pope* praised that great eighteenth-century poet for his excelling in a species of poetry "for which our author's genius was particularly turned, the didactic and the moral" (1782 ed., 1.3.101). Yet just less than one biblical lifetime later, three score and ten years, minus two, in 1824 Thomas Dibdin was writing in his influential and massive handbook to literature, the impressively titled *Library Companion, or the Young Man's Guide and the Old Man's Comfort in the Choice of a Library*, of his disdain for "the dullest of all possible didactic and moral poetry" (682).

The supposition which underlies *Wordsworth and the Motions of the Mind* is that much of the cause of this development in attitude and readers' expectations has to do with Wordsworth and with his approaches to poetry and to readers. There is an irony here, for there are university students in these days who come away from an undergraduate encounter with Wordsworth having some doubts about our poet on these very grounds of didacticism. Those culminating lines of the 1850 *Prelude*, for one example, about "what we have loved, / Others will love, and we will teach them how" (14.448–49), the insistent promise that the poet's job is to "Instruct them" (14.450), those frequent reminders from

Wordsworth about the educative power, and indeed necessity, of poetry, sometimes tend to put off modern readers, at least casual readers. Many readers in our time consider themselves willing to be affected by a poet, or entertained, or even seduced. But when such readers encounter Wordsworth with his avowed intention of teaching, of instructing through poetry, they may decide either to pass him by or to read him for purposes other than his expressed intentions, enjoying his art somehow while remaining at least somewhat uncomfortable with his preaching.

But the greatest irony in all this is that Wordsworth is not a preacher, not really, and not at his best. His best poems are seldom very good sermons. It is astonishing, for a poet of such reputation, how seldom he is epigrammatic. He is unusually wise, but he is rarely proverbial. His teaching, and he is an avowed teacher, is of a radically different sort from the typical didacticism which preceded him. When one thinks of so good a poem, so quoted and familiar and memorable a poem, so didactic a poem, as Alexander Pope's *Essay on Man*, one realizes that Wordsworth could probably not have written such a poem, and that he would not have wanted to. Like most others in the late eighteenth century he would probably have believed that Pope had taken this richly aphoristic vein of poetry as far as it could honestly be taken; Wordsworth *had* to do something else.

Here, then, is a considerable shift in taste, and we, as heirs of the shift, should take a hard and understanding look at its origins—and at Wordsworth's role in effecting the change.

In general, we can make one fundamental distinction by noting that those lines from the last page of *The Prelude* tell us that Wordsworth is promising Coleridge that together they will teach their readers not *what* but *how*:

What we have loved,
Others will love, and we will teach them how;
Instruct them how . . .

(14.448–50)

This promise to teach his readers *how* to love, or *how* to think, and not *what* to think, goes to the heart of Wordsworth's ideas about poetic education. Yet his theories of education, and his practices, are so complicated, so varied, and are subject to such development and refining during his long poetic career, that it will be necessary to approach them through a variety of works in different styles, with different purposes, from different periods of the poet's life. The aim is to illuminate in what ways and how many ways Wordsworth showed how thoughtful he was about what he perceived as his role as an educator.

In fact, talk of education is everywhere in Wordsworth's poetry. But it is talk that is constantly tempered, talk that seems to say, "When I speak of teaching, I do not mean what is usually meant." In Book Thirteen of the 1850 *Prelude*, for example, he speaks of being

convinced at heart
How little those formalities, to which
With overweening trust alone we give
The name of Education, hath to do
With real feeling and just sense.

(13.168–72)

Never mind the grammar ("Formalities . . . hath") here. The idea is a familiar one in Wordsworth, for whom "the dazzling show" of formal education in his university days at Cambridge rather quickly reached a point where it "Had ceased to dazzle" (3.90–91). Far superior to formal schooling in their teaching power were the public roads of England, for example—but what the student learned there on the highways was not that which schoolteachers teach, and the methods of learning employed by the student were not the methods of formal education:

> When I began to enquire,
> To watch and question those I met, and speak
> Without reserve to them, the lonely roads
> Were open schools in which I daily read
> With most delight the passions of mankind,
> Whether by word, looks, sighs, or tears, revealed.
> (13.159–64)

Similarly, in a setting where crowded streets replaced lonely roads, the poet tells of his schooling in London (in *Prelude* 7), schooling that depended on "sundry and most widely different modes / Of education" (7.738–39). In seeing how Wordsworth believed he himself learned, we can begin to see how he intended to teach his readers.

"One impulse from a vernal wood" begins the famous and indeed revolutionary stanza in the poem that Lord Byron, for one, never forgave and which he ridiculed in his *English Bards and Scotch Reviewers* more than a decade after it first appeared. But Wordsworth insisted on saying it:

> One impulse from a vernal wood
> May teach you more of man,
> Of moral evil and of good,
> Than all the sages can.
> ("The Tables Turned" 21–24)

Wordsworth certainly knew that whichever may teach *more*, woodland impulses or publishing sages, they do not teach the *same*. The Ten Commandments, to take one fine example of bookish sagacity, are much more *explicit* about some of the activities which constitute moral evil and good than all the vernal impulses ever can be. But vernal woodland impulses are not didactic, in the usual sense, though they do teach. And it is this natural teaching that the poet not only has learned so greatly from and which he so highly praises but which he also seeks to imitate in his own poetic teaching. "Come forth into the light of things, / Let Nature be your teacher"—or, about as good, let "Prophets of Nature" be your teachers, and let them "speak / A lasting inspiration" (*Prelude* 14.446-47).

The kind of education he received from the "words, looks, sighs, or tears" of strangers encountered on the lonely roads taught Wordsworth to insist on a different kind of teaching from that which the schools could give. He recognized that a lot of so-called formal education is miseducation, as he says in the next-to-last book of *The Prelude*:

> In those wanderings deeply did I feel
> How we mislead each other; above all,
> How books mislead us, seeking their reward
> From judgments of the wealthy Few, who see
> By artificial lights.
> (*Prelude* 13.206-10)

This attempt, inculcated by the schools, to "see / By artificial lights" is the perversion, as Wordsworth believed, of true learning, of coming forth into the "light of things." The poet, who was himself of course a great devourer and producer of books, retained ambivalent feelings about books. He expected his readers to see the deficiencies of many common and popular kinds of books, not only the unpoetic and nonliterary works that he continually relegates to second class in the Preface to *Lyrical Ballads*, but also a large proportion of literary works that he dismisses as "frantic novels, sickly and stupid German tragedies, and deluges of idle and extravagant stories in verse." He wanted his own writings to stand apart from such books. It pleased him in 1795 when a reader whom he did not then know could see one of his works as a different kind of writing. He was proud and pleased that that reader, who turned out to be Samuel Taylor Coleridge, had recognized in *Adventures on Salisbury Plain* a new kind of book, with what Wordsworth later claimed in *The Prelude* was

> a tone,
> An image, and a character, by books
> Not hitherto reflected.
> (13.358–60)

But Wordsworth, as avid reader and successful writer of books, was of course no enemy to book learning nor advocate of book censorship on any grounds. He speaks with great power and insight in Book Five of *The Prelude* of "what I owed to books in early life" and also points to "Their later influence" (5.606–07). What he shows, and what he consistently relies on for his own best poetic teaching, is a twofold principle. First, book learning must be integrated with Nature-learning to be successful, to be enduringly true:

> This only let me add,
> From heart-experience, and in humblest sense

Of modesty, that he, who in his youth
A daily wanderer among woods and fields
With living Nature hath been intimate,
Not only in that raw unpractised time
Is stirred to extasy, as others are,
By glittering verse; but further, doth
    receive,
In measure only dealt out to himself,
Knowledge and increase of enduring joy
From the great Nature that exists in works
Of mighty Poets. Visionary power
Attends the motions of the viewless winds,
Embodied in the mystery of words.

(5.584–97)

The second part of this principle is that even for the Nature learner, obviously, all books are not equal in value. Some educators are appropriate and some are not. Some schools succeed, but others fail. Some books are true to Nature while some are false. Wordsworth holds up as his models of excellence not all teachers and not all books but only those "things that teach as Nature teaches" (5.231). This phrase from Book Five, "things that teach as Nature teaches," seems a most valuable key to understanding how Wordsworth himself learned and how he intended his poetry to teach. We know that for him the reading of great poetry could be an overwhelming pleasure:

Oftentimes at least
Me hath such strong entrancement overcome,
When I had held a volume in my hand,

Poor earthly casket of immortal verse,
Shakespeare, or Milton, Labourers divine!
(5.161–65)

His tribute in this same context to the literary tradition that
shapes not only his own mind but the human soul of literate
mankind is powerful and fitting—even if it does come in one of
the longest and most complicated sentences in the whole *Prelude*,
a single sentence encompassing in the 1850 version over twenty-
five lines, and yet a sentence, for all its length and convolutions,
which all who live in the world of prized books must heed, and
wish *we* had uttered, and uttered so well:

Yet is it just
That here, in memory of all books which lay
Their sure foundations in the heart of man,
Whether by native prose, or numerous verse,
That in the name of all inspired souls,
From Homer the great Thunderer, from the voice
That roars along the bed of Jewish song,
And that more varied and elaborate,
Those trumpet-tones of harmony that shake
Our shores in England,—from those loftiest notes
Down to the low and wren-like warblings, made
For cottagers and spinners at the wheel,
And sun-burnt travellers resting their tired limbs,
Stretched under wayside hedge-rows, ballad tunes,
Food for the hungry ears of little ones,
And of old men who have survived their joys:
'Tis just that in behalf of these, the works,
And of the men that framed them, whether known,

Or sleeping nameless in their scattered graves,
That I should here assert their rights, attest
Their honors, and should, once for all pronounce
Their benediction; speak of them as Powers
For ever to be hallowed; only less,
For what we are and what we may become,
Than Nature's self, which is the breath of God,
Or his pure Word by miracle revealed.

(5.197–222)

But even here in this tribute to books, the poet is at some pains to fit these books into a relationship with "Nature's self." And he also suggests that a proper setting for participating in literary pleasures—such a setting as a peasant's cottage or else stretched out under wayside hedge-rows—can be beneficial. It is quite clear that books, which can so easily and so often mislead, are most to be trusted when they work hand in hand with Nature and when we read them out in Nature—as, for example, Wordsworth tells us in Book Three he read Chaucer not in a schoolroom at Cambridge nor under a tutor's gaze but "Beside the pleasant Mill of Trompington / . . . in the hawthorne shade / . . . while birds were warbling" (3.278–80). And it is notable too that Wordsworth would eventually express to Coleridge, in the penultimate book of *The Prelude*, the hope that as a poet he might be able not only to "take his way among mankind / Wherever Nature leads" (13.296–97) but also might in fact produce poetry which "may become / A power like one of Nature's" (13.311–12).

In his own education, as he repeatedly tells us, Wordsworth was highly fortunate. The "fair seed-time" of his soul provided by a childhood spent in Nature was matched by the natural book learning which Wordsworth's wise mother allowed and for which he blesses her memory in *The Prelude* discussion of books and natural education. The poet's mother knew the mind's craving for intellectual food, and she allowed her son's own nature to feed at will. She was untainted by the nervous educational theories that may have warped many of William's youthful contemporaries. She trusted in Nature and human nature to find the good even in bad books. And her son's tribute to her natural wisdom is suitably grateful and also rich in its significance for our understanding of his own theories of learning and teaching:

> Let me boldly say,
> In gratitude, and for the sake of truth,
> Unheard by her, that she, not falsely taught,
> Fetching her goodness rather from times past,
> Than shaping novelties for times to come,
> Had no presumption, no such jealousy,
> Nor did by habit of her thoughts mistrust
> Our nature, but had virtual faith that He
> Who fills the mother's breast with innocent milk,
> Doth also for our nobler part provide,
> Under His great correction and control,
> As innocent instincts, and as innocent food;
> Or draws for minds that are left free to trust
> In the simplicities of opening life
> Sweet honey out of spurned or dreaded weeds.
>
> (5.264–78)

To summarize for a moment, then, it seems clear that the poet's own experience, his own education, both formal and informal, shaped in him some definite ideas about book learning and other learning, and about teaching as it is commonly done in schools and as it could be improved upon out of the schools. Many books, he found, are perverse and misleading, though even with them the human mind, when it is freed to rely on its own nature, can find value as a bee can suck honest nectar from a poisonous plant. But the books of greatest and lasting value, the best of education that one human being can gain from another, are those inspired works, filled with "the breath of God," which "teach as Nature teaches."

And how does Nature teach? Or more to the point, what does Wordsworth believe and demonstrate about how a poet can employ Nature's aims in teaching? To find out, we can turn almost anywhere in Wordsworth's poetry, his undidactic but teaching poetry. Best for such a purpose, truest to Wordsworth's intent, are, of course, not those passages which, like those so far mentioned, simply state the poet's theories, but rather the many passages and poems rich in imagination and poetic utterance that tell of human experience. In his long addition of 1802 to the Preface to *Lyrical Ballads*, the poet gives us his famous definition of a poet, a definition which may be supposed to apply particularly well to Wordsworth himself. He is "a man speaking to men," a person who is richly and unusually endowed with sensitivity and enthusiasm and imagination and expressiveness and, perhaps most significant for our present purposes, richly endowed with the ability to conjure up in himself out of the motions of his mind "passions which are indeed far from being the same as those produced by real events, yet (especially in those parts of the general sympathy which are pleasing and delightful) do more nearly resemble the passions produced by real events, than anything which, from the motions of their own minds merely, other men are accustomed to feel in themselves"

(*Prose* 1: 138). A poet, then, stands apart from the mass of mankind by the quality and effectiveness of the motions of his mind—not necessarily by the quantity of his knowledge nor the quality of his thoughts but by the motions of his mind. And the poet's job is to provoke similarly effective motions of the mind in his readers. The poet, then, is not primarily a direct transmitter of truth. He aims at setting in motion the mind of the reader, at provoking mental activity.

To see Wordsworth in action, setting the mind in motion, we must bring our attention to a variety of specific works. The first of those to be considered is "Hart-Leap Well," chosen as a starting place for several reasons. One, it is a good poem, though somewhat neglected. Two, Wordsworth himself includes it in this topic of poetic education and mental motion by his insistent discussing of this poem in terms of "thinking hearts" and "knowledge" and by including lines like "I stood in various thoughts and fancies lost" (117) and "what this place might be I then inquired" (120). Three, "Hart-Leap Well" comes in Wordsworth's final arrangement of his poems in the middle of a batch of fascinating poems. That arrangement has been much debated and frequently abandoned, but it is still unquestionably true that Wordsworth's arrangement of his works was meticulous and is frequently useful. He himself, in his letter of 6 April 1826, to Crabb Robinson claimed that his purpose in placing the poems in the groupings and order that he chose was to "make one poem smooth the way for another" and make possible a helpful continuity in "that one poem should shade off happily into another" (*Letters, LY* 4: 440). If there is anything in these claims, then it is of particular interest to find Wordsworth grouping "Hart-Leap Well" among his Poems of the Imagination, immediately preceded there by "Resolution and

Independence" and "The Thorn" and followed by "Brougham Castle" and "Tintern Abbey"—all five of these poems reflecting poetic meditation on old age of men or monuments and physical decay and ruin, with each of the five approaching these themes in a unique way.

Wordsworth averred to Lady Beaumont that "there is scarcely one of my poems which does not aim to direct the attention to some moral sentiment, or to some general principle, or law of thought, or of our intellectual constitution" (*MY* 1: 148). And certainly "Hart-Leap Well" is not one of the rare exceptions to this claim. But Wordsworth's readers must be cautious and not overhasty in picking up on his moral sentiment or other teaching. The last two lines of this poem, for example, warn us "Never to blend our pleasure or our pride / With sorrow of the meanest thing that feels" (179–80). These lines represent a fine sentiment, if not perhaps universal in its truth at least not particularly arguable. But do they represent the poem? Are they the fitting moral of the story? Is it proper or even possible to reduce "Hart-Leap Well" to what the persona-narrator calls this "One lesson" (177)?

In fact, the poem is not thus reducible, for it is itself one of those "things that teach as Nature teaches." And "things that teach as Nature teaches" do not generally teach in one-line or two-line moral tags.

Nature herself is explicitly present in the poem; there are numerous comments on what she can, cannot, will, will not do. And there is the assurance, in the last stanza of the poem, that she is the primary teacher here, not the poem nor the poet nor the storyteller. Characters in the poem, like its readers, are taught by Nature—"Taught both by what she shows, and what conceals" (178). This is a telling phrase and a crucial idea, that Nature's teaching is done both by revealing and concealing. A poem that teaches in Nature's way must be a mixture of revealing and concealing also.

What is actually revealed in the poem is, as usual with Wordsworth, quite straightforward, as long as we stick with only the overt revelations. The poem is actually two short stories. One is the almost casual tale of a traveler who narrates his own adventure and who, like every poetic persona, both is and is not the poet himself. The traveler on horseback tells of coming alone and by chance upon a sight which arrests his attention and his movement. The sight is not particularly impressive and could easily be passed without notice:

> It chanced that I saw standing in a dell
> Three aspens as three corners of a square;
> And one, not four yards distant, near a well.
> (102–04)

This rather unremarkable spot, however, does capture the questioning interest of the traveler: "What this imparted I could ill divine" (105). And when he stops he sees more; the scene becomes more interesting once it is studied and pondered:

> And, pulling now the rein my horse to stop,
> I saw three pillars standing in a line,—
> The last stone-pillar on a dark hill-top.
>
> The trees were grey, with neither arms nor head;
> Half wasted the square mound of tawny-green;
> So that you just might say, as then I said,
> "Here in old time the hand of man hath been."
> (106–12)

It is not the scene so much as the progression of ideas in the mind of the traveler that calls the attention of readers. First he sees three trees forming a right angle, then a fourth, "near a well." He stops to examine them and sees from his stopping place three stone pillars in a row leading to the top of the hill. Then he sees that the trees which had originally stopped him are dead—leafless, armless, headless. And the grass within the area they enclose is unhealthy—"Half wasted," "tawny green." The man-made pillars and the dying or dead plant life combine to tell the traveler one thing: "Here in old time the hand of man hath been." In reality, how many people actually think this way? Wordsworth never attempts to depict this traveler as Universal Man. The scene, the traveler, the response all seem by chance. Most of us who see a dead tree or two or three, and dying grass, do not instantly think of "the hand of man." And if we see a stone pillar, or even three in a row, we may suspect a human cause but not necessarily an ancient one—"in old time." It is not that the traveler's response to the scene is impossible or mistaken, just not particularly usual, not universal.

But this traveler has opened within himself a progression of thoughts, a series of mental motions, that still continues:

> I looked upon the hill both far and near,
> More doleful place did never eye survey;
> It seemed as if the spring-time came not here,
> And Nature here were willing to decay.
>
> (113–16)

A remarkable mental process! He sees first three trees, then a fourth, then three stone pillars; he sees that the trees are dead and the grass beneath them dying. Now he sees that the plant life of the whole area, not merely within the trees which earlier seemed distinctive, is blighted, and he concludes that it is a place where springtime never comes and where Nature behaves, well, unnaturally. Here, he decides, after perhaps five minutes of contemplation from atop a horse, is one place on earth where the annual seasons fail and where Nature does not renew herself.

And what does the reader decide? What do we learn? Whatever else, we realize with a start that the poem is more about *human* nature than external Nature. And we begin to question not only the narrator's responses but our own mental processes.

But the story of this traveler, who does not quite function either as poet or Greek chorus, who does not quite represent readers but who does involve us in his methods of thinking, takes up relatively little space in the poem. The other story in the poem is that which is told now by the second character to appear. He is either a "Shepherd" (121) or else just a man "in shepherd's garb attired" (118)—one of those little ambiguous details that can annoy us in Wordsworth for its evasiveness, unless we remember in time that natural teaching is done both by revealing and by concealing.

This second story is the tale of the medieval knight, Sir Walter of Wensley Moor, and his single-minded pursuit of a doomed deer, with the aftermath of that hunting party and the addition of modern comments on all this by the one dressed like a shepherd. Curiously—and powerfully—the description of this deer hunt comes first in the poem; we hear most of what the traveler hears from the shepherd before we ever meet either the traveler or the shepherd, so that at first reading the story of Sir Walter seems to be told directly to us by the poet–narrator; only when we are more than halfway through the poem on a first reading do we realize that we have got the point of view all wrong. There is, then, a conscious distancing in the poem between the medieval Sir Walter and the general narrator of the poem. Certainly, the modern shepherd seems very knowing; he knows how Sir Walter looked and how he sounded those hundreds of years ago, what words he spoke, what were the names of his hunting dogs, how many times he changed horses, what were his feelings when he stood alone over the dead deer, what he planned to build and the details of how he carried out those plans, and a good deal about his subsequent life and death.

Such detailed knowledge after a lapse of centuries, if possible at all, is certainly remarkable. But there are gaps also in the shepherd's knowledge: how did the deer die, for example?—a question that goes to the heart of the narration of this unparalleled deer hunt, but a question the shepherd evades with the line, "Nor will I mention by what death he died" (250). And the shepherd–storyteller, who knows all about the structures erected and the activities engaged in at this spot in times of old, seems uncertain even about the trees which first attracted the traveler's attention: "these lifeless stumps of aspen wood— / Some say that they are beeches, others elms" (125–26). This remarkable store of knowledge in the shepherd, coupled with some remarkable gaps in that knowledge, has a lot to do with why he seems to think, as he tells us, that "such race, I think, was never seen before" (16) and "This chase it looks not like an earthly chase" (27). We certainly are reminded, more than once, of Wordsworth's trick in other places of a narrator's raising questions, proving to us that they are interesting questions, even absorbing questions, and then refusing or being unable to answer them (see especially chapters 4 and 8, in this book).

If this mixture of knowledge and its lack in the shepherd–narrator of ''Hart-Leap Well'' is arresting, some of the things the shepherd knows without seeming to know them are even more fascinating. Let me give only a few examples. The word *doleful* is not a particular favorite with Wordsworth, though the reason for its scarcity in his poetry is certainly not that he is constantly cheerful in his expressions. There are nearly two hundred appearances of *sorrow*, for example, and its related words in Wordsworth, and close to one hundred each of both *woe* or *woeful* and of *melancholy*. But the word *doleful* appears just twenty-one times in all of his poetry. In only two poems does it appear more than once—in *The Prelude*, in widely separated uses (6.136; 9.559), and in ''Hart-Leap Well.'' And ''Hart-Leap Well'' also has one of only five appearances in all his poetry of the closely related word *dolorous*. But is ''Hart-Leap Well'' really so mournful a poem that these repetitions of *doleful* and *dolorous* actually matter? In fact, the poem is filled, at least much of the time, with eager exuberance. As Sir Walter pursues the deer it is a ''glorious day'' (8), and ''Joy sparkled in the prancing courser's eyes; / The horse and horseman are a happy pair'' (9–10), and Sir Walter hallooes and cheers his dogs on (21), and when he stands over the dead deer he gazes ''with silent joy'' (36) and congratulates himself on ''this glorious feat'' (38), for ''Never had living man such joyful lot!'' (46). Unless it can be shown that Sir Walter is simply a callous barbarian in the perversity of his joy, as indeed he generally seems not to be, the prevailing mood of the hunting tale is joy, and his decision to build what sounds very much like a miniature Xanadu to celebrate this scene of happiness seems perfectly fitting:

I'll build a pleasure-house upon this spot,
And a small arbour, made for rural joy;
'Twill be the traveller's shed, the pilgrim's cot,
A place of love for damsels that are coy.

(57–60)

Nor is Sir Walter's plan a vindictive one, designed to lord his human dominion over the defeated animal:

And gallant Stag! to make thy praises known,
Another monument shall here be raised;
Three several pillars, each a rough-hewn stone,
And planted where thy hoofs the turf have grazed.

And in the summer-time when days are long,
I will come hither with my Paramour;
And with the dancers and the minstrel's song
We will make merry in that pleasant bower.

Till the foundations of the mountains fail
My mansion with its arbour shall endure;—
The joy of them who till the fields of Swale,
And them who dwell among the woods of Ure!

(65–76)

Joy and pleasantry and love and praise—these qualities are the mood of Sir Walter's plans.

So why do *doleful* and *dolorous* appear in such a context with greater frequency than anywhere else in Wordsworth's verse? We might have to ask the shepherd, who first introduces the word *doleful*, though he probably would not know. In the midst of his description of the hunt, the happy, glorious, noisy, cheerful hunt, he says, "There is a doleful silence in the air" (12). If such a line comes as unexpected in this context, it is all the more unexpected to find, later in the poem, that the traveler has used a very similar line in his own thoughts before the shepherd even appears to tell the tale of the hunt:

> I looked upon the hill both far and near,
> More doleful place did never eye survey.
>
> (113–14)

But more unexpected still is the realization that *doleful* as it is used in these two places is not only unusual but intensely literary. Among literary antecedents to such descriptions of unparallelled dolefulness, there are two particularly noteworthy instances which Wordsworth could be expected to know but which a wandering shepherd would not—unless he were more literate, and more literately aware, than, say, John Keats, who knew Homer only by hearsay until he discovered Chapman's old translation. Wordsworth's shepherd knows too much for a shepherd. In reverse chronological order, the first of these famous uses of the word *doleful* that seems clearly antecedent to "Hart-Leap Well" comes from Homer, or more precisely from Alexander Pope's translation of *The Odyssey*, Book 23, where Odysseus tells Penelope about

> His dreadful journey to the realms beneath,
> To seek Tiresias in the vales of death;
> How in the doleful mansions he survey'd
> His royal mother, pale Anticlea's shade;
> And friends in battle slain, heroic ghosts!
>
> (23.347–51)

Antecedent to Pope's pagan netherworld mansions of dolefulness of the heroic dead here is, of course, one of Milton's most famous descriptions of his Christian Hell in Book I of *Paradise Lost*—

> No light, but rather darkness visible
> Serv'd only to discover sights of woe,
> Regions of sorrow, doleful shades, where peace
> And rest can never dwell, hope, never
> comes . . .
>
> (1.63–66)

in which, as Merritt Hughes observes, there is also the deliberate echoing of Dante's description of the entrance to the Inferno (213n). So Wordsworth's description of this once-joyous spot transformed into the most doleful, hopeless, unnatural, lifeless of places is in excellent literary company, Pope and Homer, Milton and Dante, but not the kind of company expectable from the mouths of wanderers and shepherds. The word *doleful* is all the more appropriate in these hellish settings of these poems for its ability to combine not only the usual meanings of "grieving" or "gloomy" but also the older meaning, rare by the nineteenth century certainly and therefore more bookish than current, of "crafty" and "malicious" or "deceitful"—what one would expect from "darkness visible," but probably not from a shepherd.

And Wordsworth reinforces this highly literary element of his poem by using the related, but rare for him, word *dolorous* to tell of the sounds of Nature at the site of the Hart-Leap Well; the shepherd says:

And oftentimes, when all are fast asleep,
This water doth send forth a dolorous groan.

Some say that here a murder has been done,
And blood cries out for blood.

(135–38)

All this is, after all, only the continuing effect of Sir Walter's hunting of the deer, but it is again astonishingly close to Milton's description of the grand primordial conflict between the armies of Michael and of Satan in the War in Heaven, where the heavenly hosts inflict upon Satan and his followers

pain
Implacable, and many a dolorous groan,
Long struggling underneath, ere they could wind
Out of such prison.

(*PL* 6.657–60)

The parallels are too many, too close, and too complex to be accidental. Wordsworth intentionally expresses his story of a deer hunt and its long-lasting effects in terms of epic depictions of Hell, epic struggles between good and evil.

There is a lot more here, then, than the apparent didactic tag at the end of the poem, the lesson uttered by the wanderer to the shepherd not to allow our human pleasure and pride to be based upon the suffering of an animal. Wordsworth has taken us from a deer hunt to Hell, with particular attention along the way to medieval revels and mansions and monuments, has shown us man apparently conquering Nature only to be conquered himself in the midst of his seeming grandeur, man's pride defeated and expressed in a phrase that foreshadows Shelley's

"Ozymandias": "The pleasure-house is dust:—behind, before, /
This is no common waste, no common gloom" (169–70).
We are witnesses, if not exactly to Nature's revenge, at least to
Nature's certain triumph. And we know that it is not the
exuberant and unmalicious Sir Walter that Nature both triumphs
over and in a sense redeems but all human vanity and achievement. The little Hell at the site of Hart-Leap Well will be
renewed, redeemed; Hell cannot prevail:

> But Nature, in due course of time, once more
> Shall here put on her beauty and her bloom.
>
> She leaves these objects to a slow decay,
> That what we are, and have been may be known;
> But at the coming of the milder day
> These monuments shall all be overgrown.
>
> (171–76)

The purpose in examining this poem has been, besides the
pleasure of taking another hard look at it, to observe the poet's
success in setting our minds in motion, in teaching his readers
as Nature teaches. He does so here in a variety of ways, perhaps
the chief one, with the combined effects of revealing and concealing, being a constantly renewed temptation to readers to *still*
the motions of our own minds by settling for some quick, cheap
lesson that the poem itself may briefly suggest but then resists
and does not support. We may be tempted briefly, along the way
of this poem, for example, to decide that the lesson we are being
taught is never to give up when hunting a deer, or be mag-
nanimous when you defeat a deer, or, maybe, never hunt a deer
at all, or never make hasty judgments about people who
do hunt deer, or about people who relate tales of deer hunts.

But clearly none of these lessons will do for a poem in which the poet has taken us from the pageantry and arbitrariness of medieval life to Xanadu, to Hell, to poetry and its methods, to Nature and her powers, to contemplation of the full range of human experience and human nature—"what we are, and have been" (174), and may be. The poem sets and keeps our minds in motion both while we read it and long afterward, but it is not a didactic poem; it does not tell us what to think, only that we *must* think. It does so by a series of countercurrents, conflicting views, establishing positions only to undercut them. It does not dependably present facts or theories; it educates the *heart*.

These days, maybe we are all *too* used to this kind of education. Maybe we even begin to tire in our day of hordes of people with hearts seemingly educated to sympathy but heads devoid of knowledge. Certainly it is easy for us two centuries later to miss the novelty of Wordsworth's approach to poetic education, to miss the freshness of his dream, to miss the new way he conveyed not so much information nor moral preachments but a necessity for responsive thought. But his contemporaries, the alert ones, saw what he was doing and hailed it as an artistic and educative revolution. As John Payne Collier wrote, in an 1816 review of a work by James Hogg, Wordsworth was creating a new kind of poetry which required a new kind of audience:

> There is nothing in the history of literature that gives us greater pleasure than the growing estimation of which the productions of [Wordsworth] is held. The principles upon which he started as an author were so repugnant to what had until

then almost appropriated to itself the name of poetry, that he had many difficulties and repugnances to overcome:—those who had habitually considered poetry to depend more upon the language, than upon the thought that language conveyed—who had been accustomed to admire full-sounding bombastic lines as the very quintessence of excellence—would not at first relish productions composed of *the real language of men in a state of vivid sensation,* which is the very foundation of the system of Mr. Wordsworth; they who have been used to hear the most familiar expressions tricked in the ponderous trappings of phraseology, for a time could endure nothing else; but within the last few years a rapid improvement in this respect has taken place, and the public begin to perceive that they had been misled by those who had little else but words to give them. (466–67)

Wordsworth as poet–educator achieved exactly what he wanted to do: he conveyed not so much his own thoughts or judgments but, as Collier exclaims, he conveyed the inspiration to the process of thought. In that next-to-last book of *The Prelude* where he denounces miseducation and specifically denounces "how books mislead us," he expresses his hopes for his own writings, his own books, his determination to make "verse / Deal boldly with substantial things" (13.234–35). In these stirring words, which remain substantially the same from their composition in 1804 to their publication in 1850, he writes:

haply shall I teach,
Inspire; through unadulterated ears
Pour rapture, tenderness, and hope,—my theme
No other than the very heart of man,
As found among the best of those who live,—
Not unexalted by religious faith,
Nor uninformed by books, good books, though
    few—
In Nature's presence: thence may I select
Sorrow, that is not sorrow, but delight;
And miserable love, that is not pain
To hear of, for the glory that redounds
Therefrom to human kind, and what we are.

                                        (13.238–49)

Here is the best kind of teacher—the kind we all wish we could be and have, not one who fills the student's notebook with often questionable and more often obsolescent information, but one who sets the mind in motion.

Appropriately for such a teacher, Wordsworth constantly shows himself much less concerned than major poets who preceded him with *where* these mental motions may lead us. As Robert Langbaum remarks in *The Poetry of Experience*, Wordsworth prefers "the process of formulating values" to actual arrival "at a final formulation" (26). This approach, perhaps the hardest of all for educators of wavering faith, is one that requires that most Wordsworthian of virtues, an utter and unshakable faith in the trustworthiness of the human mind and its destiny, a surety that the mind which remains in genuine motion will not for long go astray.

CHAPTER TWO

Dissimilitude, Uncertainty, and the Activity of the Mind

"Every great Poet is a Teacher; I wish either to be considered as a Teacher or as nothing." So wrote Wordsworth in 1808 to his friend and fellow artist-teacher Sir George Beaumont, in a letter particularly rich in the glimpses it offers us into the poet's intentions (*MY* 1: 195). Clearly for Wordsworth this claim to be a Teacher, or nothing at all, was central to his work. And for us, his readers and his students, it is a claim which needs clarification and understanding.

For Wordsworth can hardly be called a teacher in any ordinary sense of the term, that ordinary sense, conveyed by the *Oxford English Dictionary*, the monumental edifice of Victorian knowledge and scholarship, which defines the word *teacher* as "an instructor" and "one whose function is to give instruction, esp. in a school." And this "instruction" presented by a teacher the *OED* defines as "the imparting of knowledge or skill."

All this may indeed be a bit too uncomplicated, for it ignores the fact that very frequently Wordsworth in his poetry, that is, in his role as a Teacher, not only does not *impart* knowledge but seems bent in a curious way to undermine what we suppose to be our knowledge, even somehow to diminish our certainty that we really know something at all.

Of course, the discussion of the term *teacher* in the *OED* acknowledges that the word is often used figuratively. And the earliest use cited there is indeed figurative, from a medieval manuscript in the Bodleian Library in which Cato is quoted as saying that "Ðe gode techer, Oþere mannes liif is oure shewer."

But by the late nineteenth century when work was underway on the massive collecting of citations which underlie the *OED*, the word *teacher* seems to have become, as it generally remains today, much more narrow and specific in regular use. The dictionary citation for 1870 states that "the term 'teacher' includes . . . every person who forms part of the educational staff of a school." In such usage, teaching is professional, institutional, regulated, organized. And it is a far cry from what Wordsworth was talking about when he claimed that he, like "every great Poet," was a Teacher.

Near the end of the 1800 Preface to *Lyrical Ballads*, Wordsworth, admitting that he has been discussing a complex theory of poetry without explaining the bases of that theory, offers just a momentary view of those foundations:

> If I had undertaken a systematic defence of the theory upon which these poems are written, it would have been my duty to develope the various causes upon which the pleasure received from metrical language depends. Among the chief of these causes is to be reckoned a principle which must be well known to those who have made any of the Arts the object of accurate reflection; I mean the pleasure which the mind derives from the perception of similitude and dissimilitude. This principle is the great spring of the activity of our minds and their chief feeder. From this principle the direction of the sexual appetite, and all the passions connected with it take their origin: It is the life of our ordinary conversation; and upon the accuracy with which similitude in dissimilitude, and dissimilitude in

similitude are perceived, depend our taste and our moral feelings. It would not have been a useless employment to have applied this principle to the consideration of metre, and to have shewn that metre is hence enabled to afford much pleasure, and to have pointed out in what manner that pleasure is produced. But my limits will not permit me to enter upon this subject. (Prose 1: 148)

These claims, coming as they do from one of our most original and most perceptive theorists in the arts, demand our attention. Here in this perhaps awkward but irreplaceable phrase, the accurate perception of "similitude in dissimilitude, and dissimilitude in similitude," Wordsworth finds the key to the intellect, the emotions, social sense, artistic and aesthetic taste, and morality. He offers us, however, not information but sharpened perceptions, not what we usually call knowledge but, at least at the start of his process with us, a disconcerting uncertainty amid our own reflections.

For one of Wordsworth's discoveries in his determination to be a Teacher is that the reduction of certainty is the beginning of "the activity of our minds" and makes possible their feeding. Derek Colville, in a recent book entitled *The Teaching of Wordsworth*, writes feelingly and convincingly of this necessary beginning place for what he calls "that endlessly expanding journey into awareness that Wordsworth at his best creates" (104). This journey is not, and never has been, the general method of teaching used in schools or anywhere else. Perhaps our present situation has much to do with our non-Wordsworthian habits of learning and teaching in a culture which measures education by testing, not truth, and in which schools often regulate and fear, rather than activate and feed, the searching, probing, questioning motions of the learner's mind.

Too often readers of Wordsworth have a kind of thoughtless response to his poetic references to teaching: There goes the poet again, mixing his notions about education with his impulses from vernal woods. But such a response will not really do for long. It does not begin to be sufficiently attentive to the painstakingly precise language of the poet. In the same letter to Beaumont in which he claims for himself the title of Teacher, Wordsworth insists, and properly too, "My language is precise," and he denounces any reader who could dare to offer "'criticism or judgement founded upon and exemplified by a Poem . . . inattentively perused" (*MY* 1: 195). And still more insistently, the poet exclaims that his best expectation for praise is founded in these demands he makes on the reader's powers of close scrutiny and perception: "I have not written down to the level of superficial observers and unthinking minds" (*MY* 1: 195).

In an effort to understand what the poet is getting at in this theorizing on the educational effects of perceiving similitude amid dissimilitude, and vice versa, we can do no better than to take a "near look" at some of his poems and his efforts in them to exemplify and clarify just how he believes "the activity of our minds" is stirred.

Curiously, the *OED*, in its discussion of the term *teacher* actually cites Wordsworth among its examples of uses of the word. The citing of Wordsworth is curious because the example given is quite out of place in the midst of more ordinary and orthodox usages of *teacher*. The passage cited is from the 1807 "Song at the Feast of Brougham Castle," a poem which is somewhat neglected, but unjustly so; for as Andrew J. George observed long ago, the "Song at Brougham Castle" actually deserves to be considered among Wordsworth's best works since it is "representative of the variety of form and feeling of which Wordsworth was master" (853).

The form of the poem, which Professor George thus praises, gets us at once into the heart of the poem and also into what Wordsworth is typically aiming at. For the form of the "Song at Brougham Castle" purports to be the transmission and translation by a modern poet and commentator of the song sung by an ancient minstrel. But the chief comment from the modern narrator is that the ancient minstrel did not know what he was talking about—so that the effect of the whole is both paradox and a kind of extended oxymoron. It seems a lot of trouble to make available for modern readers a song by a minstrel who has missed the main point about that which he is singing. In fact, though, this complex self-contradiction typifies Wordsworth as Teacher.

> High in the breathless Hall the Minstrel sate,
> And Emont's murmur mingled with the Song.—
> The words of ancient time I thus translate,
> A festal strain that hath been silent long.
>
> (1–4)

And then comes the "festal strain" itself, from a minstrel of three centuries earlier who is surely one of Wordsworth's most interesting narrators and personae. Like Wordsworth, he sings in harmony with Nature, for the murmuring of the River Emont mingles with his song. And like Wordsworth, the Minstrel is sensitive to the echoing voices of Nature:

> Loud voice the Land has uttered forth,
> We loudest in the faithful north:

> Our fields rejoice, our mountains ring,
> Our streams proclaim a welcoming.
>
> (30–33)

The various castles of the Clifford family rejoice at their Lord's triumph and restoration, and above all, Brougham Castle rejoices—for "here is perfect joy and pride" (50), the kind of joy that Wordsworth himself so well expresses elsewhere when the right triumphs.

The Minstrel sings of the boy Henry Clifford, whose mother protected him during the ravages of the Wars of the Roses, when the Yorkist forces aimed at hunting down the Cliffords to extermination. Young Henry's mother disguised him as a shepherd boy. Thus disguised, "he was free to sport and play, / When falcons were abroad for prey" (100–01).

It is here that the Minstrel goes astray and misses the point of the very story he is telling. He supposes that this period as a shepherd boy was for Henry Clifford a great hardship, a durance vile, from which he was rescued by the ascension to the throne of Henry VII and the ending of Yorkist oppression. And the Minstrel supposes that it is the superior blood and breeding of a Clifford which inevitably *tells*: once a nobleman always a nobleman, even in shepherd's clothes; and when such a man is restored to his proper place of leadership, he will surely triumph in exploits of military heroism:

> Tell thy name, thou trembling Field;
> Field of death, where'er thou be,
> Groan thou with our victory!
> Happy day, and mighty hour,
> When our Shepherd in his power,

Mailed and horsed, with lance and sword
To his ancestors restored
Like a reappearing Star,
Like a glory from afar,
First shall head the flock of war!

(147–55)

Here it is that Wordsworth and his persona–Minstrel part company.

And yet not utterly. For the Minstrel knows that Clifford's period of exile was spent amid what he calls the ''sympathy'' (117) of Nature. If he was forced by harsh circumstances to pass ''a weary time'' (108), the boy was nevertheless ''a happy Youth'' (107). But the Minstrel misses the *educative* power of Nature, and in missing *that*, Wordsworth would say, misses everything.

Indeed, the Minstrel describes the boy Clifford as happy in Nature but not a part of it—much in the vein of, say, Shakespeare's Orlando in his exile in the Forest of Arden, upon whom Nature need exercise no refining power because he carries his ''gentleness'' with him wherever he goes, an innate aristocracy, an inherited and immediately recognizable quality (*AYL* 2.7.102). Says the Minstrel of the young Henry Clifford in shepherd's disguise:

His garb is humble; ne'er was seen
Such garb with such a noble mien;
Among the shepherd–grooms no mate
Hath he, a Child of strength and state!
Yet lacks not friends for simple glee,
Nor yet for higher sympathy.

To his side the fallow-deer
Came, and rested without fear;
The eagle, lord of land and sea,
Stooped down to pay him fealty.
(112–21)

This Minstrel is a fine observer of the outward appearances of Nature, but he does not, as Wordsworth says the keenest observers must, "see into the life of things" ("Tintern Abbey" 49). He can see, but not feel, the worth of Nature. And this crucial period of young Henry Clifford's education, the Minstrel ascribes to supernatural, not natural, influences and benefits. Wordsworth tells us in a note that "It is imagined by the people of the country that there are two immortal Fish" which live in Bowscale-tarn near Threlkeld (quoted in George 858n), and the Minstrel alludes to this superstition of the two immortal fish before he gives way to a downright triumphant effusion on heavenly ministrations to the young nobleman during his sojourn in the wilderness:

And both the undying fish that swim
Through Bowscale-tarn did wait on him;
The pair were servants of his eye
In their immortality;
And glancing, gleaming, dark or bright,
Moved to and fro, for his delight.
He knew the rocks which Angels haunt
Upon the mountains visitant;
He hath kenned them taking wing:
And into caves where Faeries sing
He hath entered; and been told

By Voices how men lived of old.
Among the heavens his eye can see
The face of thing that is to be;
And, if men report him right,
His tongue could whisper words of might.

(122–37)

All this sort of talk, whether of immortal fish or direct interven-
tion of Angels and Faeries or Divine Providence itself, is very
grand and lofty, of course, in its medieval-minstrel way. But it
is also false. Wordsworth concludes the poem by setting the
record straight, even though it means contradicting much of what
has gone before in the same poem. The modern poet, insisting
that the ancient Minstrel was in error, acknowledges that
Providence may have played a part in shaping Clifford's
character but did so by natural, not supernatural, influences:

Alas! the impassioned minstrel did not know
How, by Heaven's grace, this Clifford's heart was
    framed:
How he, long forced in humble walks to go,
Was softened into feeling, soothed, and tamed.
Love had he found in huts where poor men lie;
His daily teachers had been woods and rills,
The silence that is in the starry sky,
The sleep that is among the lonely hills.

(157–64)

It is, of course, these last lines which the *OED* cites in its
discussion of the word *teacher*. But observe the quandary into
which Wordsworth plunges his readers here, that Wordsworth

who himself wants "to be considered as a Teacher, or as nothing." What kinds of teachers are woods and rills and starry skies and lonely hills? What knowledge or skill or information do they impart, to what school do they belong, and how is it they teach? Such questions are not easy to answer, perhaps, but they do represent an opening of the mind for readiness to activity, a crucial first step before the feeding of the mind can even begin. In undermining our certainty of the information presented, and then contradicted, in "Brougham Castle," the poet prepares us to learn. But about all he really directly teaches us here is that in this poem he is *refusing* to convey to us reliable information, leaving us instead to ponder the irreconcilable claims of the ancient Minstrel and the modern narrator, mingling similitude and dissimilitude with the effect of activating our minds, true enough, but leaving us also in a disquieting state of uncertainty.

It is remarkable how many of Wordsworth's poems, especially his short narrative poems and his brief descriptions, work just this way. Another kind of example is the 1798 poem, later included among the Poems of the Fancy, which begins, "A whirl-blast from behind the hill / Rushed o'er the wood with startling sound," and in which, just twelve lines later, the poet tells us, "There's not a breeze—no breath of air" (1-2, 13). That is, Wordsworth begins by insisting on one of the most dramatic gusts of wind in all his poetry, only to insist with equal force a moment later that "the air was still" (3)—all as part of his presenting a scene of vibrant emotion, for "here, and there, and every where," he says,

> The leaves in myriads jump and spring,
> As if with pipes and music rare

Some Robin Goodfellow were there,
And all those leaves, in festive glee,
Were dancing to the minstrelsy.

(14, 17–21)

Unless we decide that he expects us to believe in Faeries in the form of hailstones providing music for leaves to dance to, we are left by the poet uncertain in the midst of these similitudes and dissimilitudes. But Wordsworth's object here, as so frequently, is not certainty, not information on the behavior of leaves. In lines which he added to the end of the poem for the editions of 1800–05, the poet speaks again of the ability of the poetic undermining of certainty to lead to mental activity in the observer:

Oh! grant me Heaven a heart at ease,
That I may never cease to find,
Even in appearances like these,
Enough to nourish and to stir my mind!

(*PW* 2: 128n)

And now an example from Wordsworth's later years. Written several decades after "Song at Brougham Castle" and "A whirl-blast from behind the hill," and interestingly echoic of the "whirl-blast" poem, the little poem entitled "Airey-Force Valley" is another, quite different but equally useful, example of Wordsworth the poet–Teacher revealing the difficulty of certainty, of knowledge, amid similitude and dissimilitude. The poem tells of a small mountain brook above Ullswater cascading in seeming silence through its concealed chasm. It will be useful to remember as we look at this poem, while keeping in mind the "whirl-blast" lines as well, the well-known fact that Wordsworth, like many other poets, generally—in fact, I think, in his case, *always*—used the wind of Nature as a symbol for, among other things, the Spirit of God. Meyer H. Abrams's fine essay entitled "The Correspondent Breeze" provides the definitive treatment of this theme. Thus, when the breezes and winds blow in Wordsworth's poetic descriptions, we can certainly expect them to *be* breezes, but also akin in some degree to the great Pentecostal "rushing mighty wind." Now the poem:

> —Not a breath of air
> Ruffles the bosom of this leafy glen.
> From the brook's margin, wide around, the trees
> Are steadfast as the rocks; the brook itself,
> Old as the hills that feed it from afar,
> Doth rather deepen than disturb the calm
> Where all things else are still and motionless.
> And yet, even now, a little breeze, perchance
> Escaped from boisterous winds that rage without,
> Has entered, by the sturdy oaks unfelt,
> But to its gentle touch how sensitive
> Is the light ash! that, pendent from the brow
> Of yon dim cave, in seeming silence makes
> A soft eye-music of slow-waving boughs,
> Powerful almost as vocal harmony
> To stay the wanderer's steps and soothe his
>   thoughts.
>
> (PW 2: 209)

This perfect little marvel of a poem offers fine opportunities to benefit from perceiving dissimilitude in similitude. Apparently a sole observer, the poet–narrator, his observations closely confined by the brief moment and the narrow space, simply tells us what he sees and observes here right now. But what he sees and observes is a series of total contradictions. "Not a breath of air" (we remember here the wind of Pentecost), and in that breezelessness all things are steadfast—not necessarily uninspired and lost, but steadfast. And even the brook, which, despite the image of silence and motionlessness insisted on in the poem, is a real flowing brook, a real, swift, and noisy brook—even the brook, in the poem, "Doth rather deepen than disturb the calm," doth in fact seem as immobilized as the winds. Not much, apparently, in the way of feeding or activating the mind of the reader here. Where is the poet–teacher to cause some mental stir, to disturb the all-pervasive calm?

But yet. ("I do not like 'but yet,' " says Shakespeare's Cleopatra, and we understand why; for "yet," "but yet," "and yet" always introduce disquieting dissimilitude into what seems our easily handled "still and motionless" similitude.) "And yet," says Wordsworth, after describing this totally breezeless, totally still scene, "a little breeze . . . / Has entered." We observe with some wonderment that the breeze did not enter the scene after the stillness; it is just that the poet only *mentioned* it after describing the stillness. The breeze was there simultaneously with the stillness—not "next" or "soon," but "even now." The moment encompassed by the poem—a blink of an eye, an eternity— contains within it at once both breeze and breezelessness.

And as for the breeze, what does this inspiring wind accomplish by its presence? Nothing, if you are an oak tree. Amid breezelessness the oaks are "steadfast as the rocks," and in the breeze they still remain sturdy, and the breeze remains "unfelt." Similitude, surely, in dissimilitude. But to the gentle touch of the escaping breeze, "how sensitive is the light ash!" sensitive to the point of creating "a soft eye-music of slow-waving boughs," powerful, startling, soothing—all at once.

And what if you are neither an oak nor an ash but a poet, or a reader? What does the entering of the breeze of inspiration, when there had seemed to be only stillness, do for you then? Well, by the evidence of the poem, it certainly plays havoc with your iambic pentameter, for one thing. The lines describing the seeming calm are essentially regular in their meter. But the lines descriptive of the effect of the wind on the ash tree rebuke our efforts at regular scanning. It is almost as if the meter itself refuses to be a certainty. And this metrical unpredictability seems to reach its essence in the line "Powerful almost as vocal harmony," in which the rhythmic irregularities so nicely undercut the power of the apparent denotations of the words.

Whatever is *felt* here as we respond to this lovely poem, nothing at all is *known* as a certainty, nothing taught—in the conventional sense. Is the poet recommending steadfastness, or sensitivity to the breeze? Does he want us to resolve to deepen the calm that surrounds us or to disturb it? Do we believe him when he says there is "not a breath of air" or when he simultaneously informs us that "even now, a little breeze . . . / Has entered"? Is iambic pentameter preferable to confused rhythms? Is it better to respond to whatever breeze may blow our way, like the ash, or to be sturdy and independent like an oak? The poem does not really address any of these questions, though it seems to *raise* them all. The poet again seems chiefly to teach that he will *not* teach—that is, that he will convey no message, nor certainty, nor moral—that the only thing we know from the poem is that we are uncertain—especially, here, that we are uncertain even what our own perceptions are and how those perceptions are, or are not, shaped. The chief certainty, in short, that we gain from such a poem is the sharp awareness of the absolute inevitability of our own humility. And in that state can begin fruitfully "the activity of our mind."

I stress *fruitful* mental activity. For Wordsworth, the Teacher, has promised, amid the insistence of mingling similitude and dissimilitude, not only to *activate* our minds, but to *feed* them, to supply us with, after all, knowledge. But how and where in his poetry are knowledge and certainty to be gained?

Clearly such a question calls to mind Thomas De Quincey's distinction between what he calls the literature of knowledge and the literature of power. In his essay "The Poetry of Pope," De Quincey compares the teaching done by a great poet and that done by a book of instructions:

> What do you learn from *Paradise Lost*? Nothing at all. What do you learn from a cookery-book? Something new, something you did not know before, in every paragraph. . . . What you owe to Milton is not any knowledge, of which a million separate items are still but a million of advancing steps on the same earthly level; what you owe is *power*,—that is, exercise and expansion to your own latent capacity of sympathy with the infinite, where every pulse and each separate influx is a step upwards, a step ascending as upon a Jacob's ladder from earth to mysterious altitudes above the earth. (11: 55–56)

But to cite De Quincey in this context is to return to Wordsworth, for De Quincey tells us that for this "distinction" between literature of knowledge and of power, "as for most of the sound criticism on poetry, or any subject connected with it that I have ever met with, I must acknowledge my obligations to many years' conversation with Mr. Wordsworth'' (10: 48n). Clearly in his relationship with De Quincey, Wordsworth was a successful Teacher, and De Quincey a ready student.

Much of what Wordsworth attempts as a Teacher and as a theorist upon the notion of education through poetry is in reaction to some of the teaching he received in his own formal education. He makes especially a great point of denouncing those at Cambridge who tried to force his mind without first winning his will. As he writes in *Prelude* 3, such an approach to education, and it is one of the most common of standard approaches, will always fail:

> Was ever known
> The witless shepherd who persists to drive
> A flock that thirsts not to a pool disliked?
> (3.408–10)

Not only does this kind of system of education fail in its specific intent of instilling knowledge in the students' minds; this system even teaches—and Wordsworth makes it sound as if this is *all* it teaches—the students to despise knowledge. Rather than providing a spring for the activity of minds, it shuts down mental activity:

> Even Science [that is, knowledge, general
>   learning], . . .
> In daily sight of this irreverence,
> Is smitten thence with an unnatural taint,

Loses her just authority, falls beneath
Collateral suspicion, else unknown.

(3.421–25)

Having found himself a victim of such a system of schooling, Wordsworth at first attempts to describe an ideal institu-
tion of education—"a sanctuary for our country's youth" (431),
"a primeval grove" (433), "A habitation sober and demure / For
ruminating creatures" (438–39). But he gives it up as an imprac-
tical dream and relegates the dream of such a school to some
paradisal Bartramesque setting in the exotic swamps of Florida-
cum-Xanadu, where no human element learns or thinks or
intrudes, where thinking is the activity of the birds and "the
pelican / Upon the cypress spire in lonely thought / Might sit
and sun himself" (442–44).

In fact, Wordsworth learned from his frustration at Cambridge
but also from his encounters, both in childhood and in maturity,
with books and Nature that a far better symbol for his sense of
real learning than a school classroom is a single reader with a
single book, or an individual soul in and at one with Nature.
He insists on this contrast between, on the one hand,

those with whom
By frame of Academic discipline
We were perforce connected, men whose sway
And known authority of office served
To set our minds on edge, and did no more,

(3.538–42)

and, on the other hand, real Teachers, like shepherds, for
example, away from the schools, whose source of knowledge

is "Nature's book of rudiments" and who employ Nature's "tender scheme / Of teaching comprehension with delight, / And mingling playful with pathetic thoughts" (557–61). Similitude amid dissimilitude, the great spring of mental activity.

But it would be the merest sentimentality to pretend that the complex and intensely intellectual art and sophistication of poetry can really be the same kind of Teacher as a shepherd ruminating on "the green valleys, and the streams and rocks" (*Michael* 63). Wordsworth does not and cannot pretend to be, as a poet, also and only a shepherd. Indeed he has little patience with those who make attempts at such a pretense, as he reveals in giving to Isabella Fenwick his opinion on James Hogg, the so-called "Ettrick Shepherd," who was, he said, "undoubtedly a man of original genius, but of coarse manners and low and offensive opinions" (PW 4: 459n).

Wordsworth, at least at his best and most typical, avoids the pitfalls of both the academics and the sentimentalists. He proclaims himself, just as they also proclaim themselves, a Teacher, but he finds his own unique and immensely important path to teaching. Perhaps his clearest brief statement of that path comes in his letter to Coleridge of 22 May 1815: "One of my principal aims has been . . . rather to remind men of their knowledge, as it lurks inoperative and unvalued in their own minds, than to attempt to convey recondite or refined truths" (MY 2: 238). This seems a most significant theory of teaching, with the reader or student consulting himself or herself for the source of knowledge, the poet–Teacher's task being to incite the activity of the mind which effects that interior search. Here, uncertainty becomes the crucial step towards knowledge, perhaps towards eventual certainty. And the tension between similitude and dissimilitude is the activator of the process.

The poet can also perform a further function; he does not generally convey knowledge, in the sense of information, but he can supply emphasis, or, as Wordsworth says, "direct the attention." Writing to Lady Beaumont in 1807, Wordsworth says: "There is scarcely one of my Poems which does not aim to direct the attention to some moral sentiment, or to some general principle, or law of thought, or of our intellectual constitution" (MY 1: 148). And again this "general principle" of his poetic method, as Wordsworth himself identifies it, has its basis in distinguishing dissimilitude in similitude. As he continues to Lady Beaumont: "Who is there that has not felt that the mind can have no rest among a multitude of objects, of which it either cannot make one whole [that is, by perceiving the unifying similitude amid dissimilitude], or from which it cannot single out one individual [dissimilitude amid similitude], whereupon may be concentrated the attention divided among or distracted by a multitude?" (MY 1: 148).

What Wordsworth consciously and intentionally *avoids* in all such talk of teaching and learning is any systematized institutionalizing philosophy or method of education. His educator's faith is in the individual mind, not in systems. He developed that faith through his own experience, as he tells us in The Prelude. His personal encounters with formal schooling were, as we know, both good and very bad. But his individual experiences at informal learning were the essential foundation which enabled him to find value in the good schooling and which equipped his mind to survive the bad schooling experiences.

Particularly in Prelude 5, innocently and a bit misleadingly entitled simply "Books," the poet explains this crucial foundation laid in personal experience. Before even mentioning any of

his important encounters with books, Wordsworth identifies the
essential basis for book-learning:

> My mind hath looked
> Upon the speaking face of earth and heaven
> As her prime teacher.
>
> (5.12–14)

This prime teacher is that which readies the youthful mind for
other learning and bestows on the mind a power of judgment
and discernment which enables us to transform information and
ideas and experiences into knowledge, not mere confusion. The
poet exults in the awareness that his own childhood, under the
loving care of a wise mother, gave him, as he says, one of those
"minds that are left free to trust / In the simplicities of opening
life" (5.276–77). A mind "left free to trust"—the concept may
even seem a startling one amid all the conflicting theories of
educational methods and examinations and requirements still
so much with us. And the poet places no hope in the educationalists of his own day. Instead he vows to show his gratitude
at having escaped the detrimental effects of the school systems
of a later generation, to

> pour out
> Thanks with uplifted heart, that I was reared
> Safe from an evil which these days have laid
> Upon the children of the land, a pest
> That might have dried me up, body and soul.
>
> (5.225–29)

Nor would Wordsworth have any increased faith in the
descendants of those late eighteenth-century educationalists who

are still so active in our own time. Indeed, he anticipates the huge and unrealistic claims of some modern educational methodizers, and he piles upon them a somewhat unusual passage of mocking epical scorn, even linking those theorizers with Milton's personifications of Sin and Death, the offspring of Satan himself, who, in *Paradise Lost*, like Wordsworth's educationalists undeterred by the unreality of their plans, build a bridge over chaos. Wordsworth's allusion is typically both concise and aslant—he makes only a brief mention of those who pretend to "have overbridged . . . chaos"—but in doing so he brings powerfully to mind Milton's vivid image of the vulture-like character of Death, who, like Wordsworth's educational schemers, "upturn'd / His Nostril wide into the murky Air, / Sagacious of his Quarry" (*PL* 10.279–81), and of the combined efforts of Sin and Death, who, Milton says, achieve "a passage broad, / Smooth, easy, inoffensive down to Hell" (*PL* 10.304–05). For Wordsworth, the earthly counterparts of Milton's grim pair are the schoolmen:

> These mighty workmen of our later age,
> Who, with a broad highway, have overbridged
> The froward chaos of futurity,
> Tamed to their bidding; they who have the skill
> To manage books, and things, and make them act
> On infant minds as surely as the sun
> Deals with a flower; the keepers of our time,
> The guides and wardens of our faculties,
> Sages who in their prescience would control
> All accidents, and to the very road
> Which they have fashioned would confine us down,
> Like engines; when will their presumption learn,

That in the unreasoning progress of the world
A wiser spirit is at work for us,
A better eye than theirs, most prodigal
Of blessings, and most studious of our good,
Even in what seem our most unfruitful hours?

(5.347-63)

To speak thus of a "wiser spirit" that works for our genuine education, in contrast to the confining efforts of schoolmen and educationalists, is typically Wordsworthian—one of those understated, easy-to-miss, seemingly vague, seemingly evasive phrases, which, in fact, upon reconsideration, contains the poet's whole point on the subject. For this "wiser spirit" is within each individual, and only in it can we place our educational trust. Here is the ultimate example of similitude amid dissimilitude. Here too, for Wordsworth, is the reliable source of Knowledge, what he insistently calls "knowledge, rightly honoured with that name— / Knowledge not purchased by the loss of power!" (5.424-25).

The poet's role as Teacher, then, is based not only in self-confidence but above all in confidence in the mind of the individual human being. The poet–Teacher engages the mind of the reader but need not, in the usual method of education, convey information or knowledge. Wordsworth asks only that his student–reader first possess an attitude of humility, an *un*certainty. To such a student the poet–Teacher offers, first, a call to attention, a fixing of attention, and then an urging to mental activity, a rousing. At this point, Wordsworth's faith in the human mind, his own and his reader's, takes over in the teaching process. As he wrote to Lady Beaumont, "The mind being once fixed and rouzed, all the rest comes from itself"

(*MY* 1: 149). And once the mind is set in motion by the poet's efforts, the direction of its activity can be trusted, for it is governed, says Wordsworth in *Prelude* 5, by "nothing less, in truth, / Than that most noble attribute of man" (572–73), that human quality which is the very basis of Wordsworth's theories and understanding of human nature and certainly the principle which leads him to assert that "Every great Poet is a Teacher," and the foundation of his assurance that he would finally come "to be considered as a Teacher, or as nothing." It is no less an assertion of idealism than this: that the mind of man, which is the poet-Teacher's workplace, even when it is "yet untutored and inordinate," is always at its base governed by

> That wish for something loftier, more adorned,
> Than is the common aspect, daily garb,
> Of human life.
>
> (5.574–77)

Here Wordsworth stakes his banner of faith. Here he is the Teacher.

CHAPTER THREE

Flashes of Surprise: Wordsworth and the Princes of Serendip

"I once read a silly fairy tale," wrote Horace Walpole to Horace Mann, "called *The Three Princes of Serendip*: as their highnesses traveled, they were always making discoveries, by accidents and sagacity, of things which they were not in quest of" (408–09). From this encounter with the Dutch edition of a French translation of the Italian adaptation of the thirteenth-century Persian poem which tells of the travels and adventures of these three princes of Ceylon, or Serendip, Walpole coined the word *serendipity*, which, as he boasted in this same letter to Horace Mann, is "a very expressive word" (407), useful for describing what appears to be "*accidental sagacity* (for you must observe that *no* discovery of a thing you *are* looking for comes under this description)" (408).

Serendipity, that "very expressive word," is the appropriate label for some of the very greatest of human discoveries which have come by surprise, from Columbus's encounter with America to Newton's with the apple to Alexander Fleming's with penicillin. And serendipity has its literary users and admirers too. Keats's discovery of Chapman's old translation of Homer reminded him of the serendipitous look of "wild surmise" with which Balboa and his men (alas, not Cortez) looked at each other, "Silent, upon a peak in Darien," after first seeing the Pacific Ocean.

But perhaps nobody in English poetry is so subject to moments of serendipity, flashes of surprise, as Wordsworth, who seems never to have used the word, but who ranks right up

there with the original Princes of Serendip in Walpole's "silly
fairy tale," who "were always making discoveries, by accidents
and sagacity, of things which they were not in quest of." For
Wordsworth was always doing that too. Furthermore, he often
allows his readers not merely to read about but also to *experience*
such serendipitous discoveries in his writings. Although
Wordsworth was often a very effective seeker, still it is interesting to observe in his poetic records how very frequently some
of his most sincere and energetic quests did not lead to their
expected goals, and, further, how frequently some of his most
important discoveries, as well as a large number of seemingly
trivial surprises, came by serendipity, came when they were not
directly sought. Much of his success as a learner, a discoverer
of truth, lay in his ability and willingness to see and accept truth
whether he came to it full of expectation or by surprise. This
twin willingness both to seek goals and to accept astonishments
is, he claimed, crucial to poetic genius. But by implication, it is
required too, according to the poet, of every kind of learner in
every method of education:

> From Nature doth emotion come, and moods
> Of calmness equally are Nature's gift:
> This is her glory; these two attributes
> Are sister horns that constitute her strength.
> Hence Genius, born to thrive by interchange
> Of peace and excitation, finds in her
> His best and purest friend; from her receives
> That energy by which he seeks the truth,
> From her that happy stillness of the mind
> Which fits him to receive it when unsought.
>
> (1850 *Prelude* 13.1–10)

Examples of chance discoveries are everywhere in his poetry and prose. "Resolution and Independence," for example, is a work filled with chance, based on dejection unearned and recovery unsought. Of course there *can* be profound and perhaps inescapable causes for despondency, but Wordsworth here insists on selecting mere chance as the basis for the dejection treated in this poem, almost as if the very root of "despondency and madness" is the "gladness" with which our youth begins (48–49). And then comes the encounter with the almost primeval leech-gatherer, which not only cures the present woe but remains as a source of strength for future trials. But this abundant solution to the sorrow which precedes it is not only unsought but, perhaps, even unwanted; the dejected traveller seems to look only for causes, not solutions, for disquietude and misery, and he seems to enjoy being thus miserable, wrapped in "the fear that kills; / And hope that is unwilling to be fed" (113–14). But serendipity intervenes. A chance discovery comes. The *causes* of the chance are only briefly and inconclusively contemplated before the discovery itself fills the mind of both traveller and reader:

> Now, whether it were by peculiar grace,
> A leading from above, a something given,
> Yet it befell, that, in this lonely place,
> When I with these untoward thoughts had striven
> Beside a pool bare to the eye of heaven
> I saw a Man before me unawares:
> The oldest man he seemed that ever wore grey hairs.
> (50–56)

It is both curious and important that the traveller of this poem expresses no astonishment, no sense of surprise, at this encounter with the old man. The leech-gatherer will come to figure in his thinking almost like a divine messenger come from beyond the earth, almost a redirecting and comforting angel— "like a man from some far region sent, / To give me human strength, by apt admonishment" (111-12). But the traveller never shows any amazement at this unexpected turn of events. It is the leech-gatherer alone who experiences "a flash of mild surprise" (90). Essential in Wordsworth's treatment of this instance of serendipity is not only the encounter with the unsought and the unexpected but the insistent appearance of the encounter's creating no sense of wonder in the transformed traveller—as if the unsought miraculous were perfectly expectable after all.

So often do these discoveries of things he is "not in quest of" come up in Wordsworth's writings that it is easy, after awhile, to imagine him, as in a sense he seems to have imagined himself, the very Crown Prince of Serendip. There is in him, in fact, an apparent cultivating of the "hey-day of astonishment"—the phrase is from one of the Poems on the Naming of Places addressed "To Joanna" (67). But the astonishment is sometimes conjured up, not stumbled upon, and the ultimate astonishment is likely to be within the reader instead of the poet. So, in these lines "To Joanna," we read of a girl who "Amid the smoke of cities" passed "The time of early youth" (1-2), who, transplanted briefly to the Lakes and accompanying the poet on one of his walks into the hills, sees him fall into a Wordsworthian trance, a rapture, at the sight of which she "laughed aloud" (53). The poet remains calm, seemingly untouched either by Joanna's laughter or by what follows next, though even the inanimate elements of surrounding Nature are startled into "a loud uproar in the hills" (73):

The Rock, like something starting from a sleep,
Took up the Lady's voice, and laughed again;
That ancient Woman seated on Helm-crag
Was ready with her cavern; Hammar-scar,
And the tall Steep of Silver-how, sent forth
A noise of laughter; southern Loughrigg heard,
And Fairfield answered with a mountain tone;
Helvellyn far into the clear blue sky
Carried the Lady's voice,—old Skiddaw blew
His speaking-trumpet;—back out of the clouds
Of Glaramara southward came the voice;
And Kirkstone tossed it from his misty head.

(54–65)

This wonderful description of the rocks and hills and mountain peaks, first nearby, then farther and yet farther away, echoing the sounds of jollity in a very frenzy of reverberation, is similar in sound and power to the echoing of ghostly bells in *Christabel* from Langdale Pike and Dungeon-ghyll all the way to Borodale. Certainly, this kind of reverberation fascinated Wordsworth. He was aware of the tradition stretching back to the Ancients, Greek and Hebrew, which made echoes seem to possess a divinely prophetic quality.

Let us review that tradition briefly. The seventeenth-century English Neoplatonist Henry Reynolds, for one quick example, claimed that "Pythagoras propounded his ideas in 'figurative, tipick and symbolick Notions; among which, one of his documents is this—*While the winds breathe, adore Ecco.*' " And Reynolds continues: "This *Winde* is . . . the Symbole of the Breath of God; and Ecco, the Reflection of this divine breath, or Spirit upon us; or . . . *the daughter of the divine voice;* which through the beautifying splendor it shedds and diffuses through the Soule, is justly worthy to be reverenced and adored by us" (Hollander 16). And Wordsworth's fascination with this "daughter of the divine voice," identical to the ancient Hebrew rabbinic *bat kol* ("daughter of a voice," or "echo" in modern Hebrew), was lifelong. His awareness of the long tradition underlying these divine poetic echoes is made clear in the marvelous poem called "On the Power of Sound," written at Rydal Mount almost three decades after the lines "To Joanna." There Wordsworth gives what John Hollander, in his superb little book entitled *The Figure of Echo*, calls a virtual summation of this serendipitous tradition of the indirect echoing voice of God, a summation of "the mythological history of echo" (19):

> Ye voices, and ye Shadows
> And Images of voice—to hound and horn
> From rocky steep and rock-bestudded meadows
> Flung back, and, in the sky's blue caves, reborn—
> On with your pastime! till the church-tower bells
> A greeting give of measured glee;
> And milder echoes from their cells
> Repeat the bridal symphony.
>
> (32–40)

But now, to return to the poem "To Joanna," we find depicted an astonishing and unexpected outcome to the unaffected laughter of a city girl caught off guard by Wordsworth's rural rapture over Nature. Yet, remarkably, through it all, as the mountains hurl back their divine echoing laughter from many miles around, the poet seems almost indifferent, almost unhearing. These wild echoes of Joanna's laughter, Wordsworth admitted years later to Isabella Fenwick, were "an extravagance; though the effect of the reverberation of voices in some parts of the mountains is very striking" (PW 2: 487). But the extravagance is only beginning, as is the complexly serendipitous effect of these lines on the reader. Not only was Joanna Hutchinson, Mary's nineteen- or twenty-year-old sister at the time, not reared "amid the smoke of cities," but she may not have even visited the Wordsworths in Grasmere yet, and certainly had not done so under the conditions described in the poem.

In an entry in one of his notebooks, the poet reveals candidly that the whole experience was concocted for the benefit of the Vicar in the poem, that is, the listener, or, by extension, the reader—for *us*. The true serendipity here is not described but *induced*. It is experienced not by the poet but by the reader. In this notebook entry, the poet acknowledges with extended irony his intention "in a certain degree to divert or partly play upon the Vicar" (and the reader) with an ongoing process during which his "mind partly forgets its purpose," then "entirely" loses sight of its "first purpose." And then, he says, "I am caught in the trap of my own imagination," and then "I take fire" and "terminate the description in tumult" only to "waken from the dream and see that the Vicar thinks I have been extravagating, as I intended he should," and to conclude in a "mingling" of "allusions suffused with humour, partly to the trance in which I have been, and partly to the trick I have been playing" (PW 2: 487). And all this, following a tranquillity and a recollection, is made permanent in chiselled letters in stone eighteen months afterward when, Wordsworth tells us in lines which underscore the sense of the unexpected and of truth unsought, which flows through the whole poem,

> I chanced to walk alone
> Beneath this rock, at sunrise, on a calm
> And silent morning.
>
> (78–80)

Such rewarding "chances" are one of the most constant features of Wordsworth's poetry, though the divine echoing voice of these passages, while it is a favorite Wordsworthian device, is not a necessary ingredient in the poet's frequent descriptions of, and inducements to, serendipity.

Encounters with truth unsought abound in *The Prelude*, naturally enough. It is clear that Wordsworth believed that one of the main ways in which the minds of poets and readers grow is through confronting the unexpected. It is perfectly appropriate, then, that *The Prelude* tells us that Wordsworth's childhood of natural education very often involved the unexpected:

> Even then I felt
> Gleams like the flashing of a shield;—the earth
> And common face of Nature spake to me
> Rememberable things; sometimes, 'tis true,
> By chance collisions and quaint accidents.
>
> (1850, 1.585–89)

Examples which he gives us of these chance collisions and quaint accidents include the discovery made by the boy who sets out to rob birds' nests high on a cliff but who ends up, as if following Mark Antony's advice, finding a "new heaven, new earth" (*Ant.* 1.1.17). "[T]hough mean / Our object and inglorious," the poet says, "yet the end / Was not ignoble" (1.328–30). Note that this distinction, even contrast, between objectives and ends,

between aims and results, is the essence of serendipity. The poet
continues:

> Oh! when I have hung
> Above the raven's nest, by knots of grass
> And half-inch fissures in the slippery rock
> But ill-sustained, and almost (so it seemed)
> Suspended by the blast that blew amain,
> Shouldering the naked crag, oh, at that time
> While on the perilous ridge I hung alone,
> With what strange utterance did the loud dry wind
> Blow through my ear! the sky seemed not a sky
> Of earth—and with what motion moved the
> clouds!
>
> (1.330–39)

Another such example of serendipity is given in the experience
of the dizzied boy, skating on the frozen lake, who cuts "across
the reflex of a star" (1.450) and succeeds unexpectedly in achiev-
ing a kind of instantaneous isolation not only from his friends
but from the very earth:

> Then at once
> Have I, reclining back upon my heels,
> Stopped short; yet still the solitary cliffs
> Wheeled by me—even as if the earth had rolled
> With visible motion her diurnal round!
> Behind me did they stretch in solemn train,
> Feebler and feebler, and I stood and watched
> Till all was tranquil as a dreamless sleep.
>
> (1.456–63)

A third example from the poet's childhood is the Boy of Winander, whose story Wordsworth originally tells in the first person, that haunting and unforgettable encounter with a seren- dipitous shock of silent surprise which comes amid

                                    a wild scene
Of mirth and jocund din. And when it chanced
That pauses of deep silence mocked my skill,
Then often in that silence, while I hung
Listening, a sudden shock of mild surprize
Would carry far into my heart the voice
Of mountain torrents; or the visible scene
Would enter unawares into my mind
With all its solemn imagery, its rocks,
Its woods, and that uncertain heaven, received
Into the bosom of the steady lake.
(Ms. JJ—see MS Drafts and Fragments in Norton
ed., 492, lines 14-24)

And so it goes with Wordsworth, not only in his childhood but throughout *The Prelude*—the vision which follows a "perus- ing, so it chanced" (5.59) of *Don Quixote*; the equally seren- dipitous "fortunate chance," as he calls it (6.577), of meeting a peasant on the descent from the Simplon Pass; the chance finding on the crowded streets of London of a blind beggar who wears "a written paper, to explain / His story" (7.641-42)—a sight which catches the poet's mind and turns it "round / As with the might of waters" (7.643-44); more impressively, the "one decisive rent" (10.301) with which, the poet tells us, no other shock he ever experienced can compare, by which England's leaders, in their treatment of Revolutionary France, transformed Wordsworth's native patriotism into "Change and subversion from that hour" (10.268). The climax of all these and numerous other unexpected encounters with truths unsought comes in the ascent of Mt. Snowdon. Amid all the often furious academic discussion of those lines in the concluding book of *The Prelude,* one point that often gets lost is the *serendipitous* nature of the experience. The plan that Wordsworth says he had for his climb of Mt. Snowdon was never fulfilled; it was instead replaced by something unexpected, and much better. The plan itself, as he describes it, seems rather odd and probably unlikely of success: the poet, his friend Robert Jones, and a shepherd-guide—"a trusty guide" (14.9) and "conductor" (14.17), who however apparently brings up the rear of the little procession—depart at bedtime, in the fog, and head westward, all in order to see the sun rise. If the sun never does rise in this narration, though it had earlier in a similar description in *Descriptive Sketches,* who can be surprised? But the sunrise which never occurs in *The Prelude* does not even matter:

> For instantly a light upon the turf
> Fell like a flash, and lo! as I looked up,
> The Moon hung naked in a firmament
> Of azure without cloud, and at my feet
> Rested a silent sea of hoary mist.
> (14.38–42)

And the poet, without the benefit or need of mere sunrise, witnesses a vision of light, of creation, and of "a majestic intellect" (14.67), a splendid culmination to the long process of the discoveries of a poet's mind. This supreme moment, and the supremely fine poetry in which it is couched, is surely one of the grandest triumphs of Wordsworthian serendipity in its depiction of a great and sudden and unexpected achievement, an achievement so great that it blots out all disappointment over the goal which was not reached, indeed blots out the very goal itself in the brilliant flash of the moon which overpowers the expected sunlight.

Yet another splendid poetic treatment of serendipity is in those two Poems Founded on the Affections which Wordsworth published as companion pieces. In the first of these, "The Brothers," he tells of Leonard Ewbank, the sailor home from the sea, whose loyalty and longing for home survive the misadventures of the seafarer and even "slavery among the Moors / Upon the Barbary coast" (317–18). But the ominous transformation in the face worn by Nature is too much for him, though regarded as a commonplace by the residents of Ennerdale:

> On that tall pike
> (It is the loneliest place of all these hills)
> There were two springs which bubbled side by
>   side,
> As if they had been made that they might be
> Companions for each other: the huge crag
> Was rent with lightning—one hath disappeared;
> The other, left behind, is flowing still.
> For accidents and changes such as these,
> We want not store of them.
>
> (139–47)

Such an "accident" and "change," along with all that it represents, even though it seems to the townsfolk so common as to be almost expectable, overwhelms Leonard, sends him off to sea forever, transforms him indeed into an ancient "grey-headed Mariner" (435). Such is the tragic serendipity of "The Brothers," the poem that Coleridge praised as "that model of English pastoral, which I have never yet read with unclouded eye" (*BL*, ed. Shawcross 2: 62).

In the companion poem, that wonderful but not so much read work entitled "Artegal and Elidure," written, according to Wordsworth in his comment to Miss Fenwick, "as a token of affectionate respect for the memory of Milton" (*PW* 2: 468), there is a yet stronger sense of serendipity, of unsought-for and unexpected transformation, whose only motive seems to be the chance discovery that sets it in motion. Milton had related the story of these *ancient* brothers in his *History of Britain*, and it is Milton who says that the brothers whom Wordsworth calls Artegal and Elidure "chanced to meet" after a drastic five-year separation seemingly inevitable, and inherent in the natural antipathy of good and evil. But Wordsworth puts their chance meeting in a context of a string of unlooked-for events. One surprise follows another, until, in the poem's serendipitous culmination, even these primeval opposites are reconciled. As Wordsworth, generally following Milton's account, tells the tale, King Gorbonian, unsurpassed as "Worthy of respect and love" (66), dies and leaves his throne to his elder son Artegal, who proves to be an unpleasant surprise to his subjects, and who himself is surprised by a successful revolution. Artegal,

> But how unworthy of that sire was he!
> A hopeful reign, auspiciously begun,
> Was darkened soon by foul iniquity.
> From crime to crime he mounted, till at length

> The nobles leagued their strength
> With a vexed people, and the tyrant chased;
> And on the vacant throne his worthier Brother
>   placed.
>
> (75–81)

There are surprises along the way for the reader, too. Wordsworth, that frequently stern denunciator of tyranny and oppression, treats the deposed tyrant Artegal with unexpected mildness and describes him in his wanderings as a "humbled Exile" (82) who sounds a lot like that scriptural beggar whose need for sympathetic love tests the very goodness in man, the Prodigal Son.

> Him, in whose wretched heart ambition failed,
>   Dire poverty assailed;
> And, tired with a slights his pride no more could
>   brook,
> He towards his native country cast a longing look.
>
> (86–89)

Now the surprises quickly multiply. King Elidure the Pious, out hunting "the tusky wild boar" (109), sounds the hunting horn. And, all unplanned, Artegal, we are told, "chanced to hear" the "startling outcry" (107–08). Elidure, certainly, has no anticipation of the encounter. If, as he says, his brother Artegal has been in those years often in his prayers, he has surely not been in Elidure's conscious plans, and the penultimate moment is characterized by "seeming unconcern and steady countenance" (113). But then comes the encounter:

> The royal Elidure, who leads the chase,
> Hath checked his foaming courser:—can it be!

Methinks that I should recognise that face,
Though much disguised by long adversity!
He gazed rejoicing, and again he gazed,
    Confounded and amazed—
"It is the king, my brother!" and, by sound
Of his own voice confirmed, he leaps upon the
    ground.

(114–21)

Though Elidure is as astonished as "the astonished Artegal"
(138) at this unexpected reunion, he has no doubts about its
cause. Wordsworth's traveller in "Resolution and Independence" could wonder vaguely and inconclusively "whether"
the encounter with the leech-gatherer "were by peculiar
grace, / . . . a something given" (51). But Elidure has no time
for doubts and wondering: "By Heavenly Powers conducted,
we have met" ("Artegal" 130), he affirms. Milton, in his version,
makes much of the fact that here fraternal love overcomes the
attractions and temptations of monarchal power: "a crown, the
thing that so often dazzles and vitiates mortal men, for which
thousands of nearest blood have destroyed each other, was in
respect of brotherly dearness, a contemptible thing" (PW 2: 469).
Wordsworth follows his Miltonic source faithfully, but with
a choice of words emphasizing, as Milton does not, the New
Testament parallels:

Thus was a Brother by a Brother saved;
With whom a crown (temptation that hath set
Discord in hearts of men till they have
    braved
Their nearest kin with deadly purpose met)

'Gainst duty weighed, and faithful love, did seem
A thing of no esteem.

(234–39)

The ultimate earthly serendipity is here achieved, reflecting the
ultimate act of universal serendipity, to which we shall return
later. Wordsworth's poem depicts a world in which men battle
for power, for wealth, for conquest. Human hearts are filled with
discord. And then comes Elidure, who not only loves his brother
above all earthly pursuits and distractions but who, by the power
of this love, rescues Artegal from "clouds of disgrace" (195) and
the "veil of noontide darkness" (197) and transforms him into
"Earth's noblest penitent; from bondage freed / Of vice"
(229–30). It is, in human affairs, the almost utterly unexpected,
"this triumph of affection pure" (240).

And yet it is important to observe another frequent and
fascinating ingredient in Wordsworth's treatments of serendipity.
There is often in him a haunting sense of mystery and paradoxical unconscious anticipation to accompany the serendipitous surprises. For example, the very poetic and lovely language which
he employs in prose to describe his response to the military and
political astonishments that he experienced during the early
Napoleonic Era exemplify the haunting and the mysterious and
paradoxical awareness of unconscious anticipation. As he writes
in 1808 in his *Convention of Cintra* tract about the treaty which
British generals had made in Portugal with Napoleon's representatives, the poet says,

Yet was the event by none received as an open
and measurable affliction: it had indeed features
bold and intelligible to every one; but there was

an under-expression which was strange, dark, and mysterious—and, accordingly as different notions prevailed, or the object was looked at in different points of view, we were astonished like men who are overwhelmed without forewarning—fearful like men who feel themselves to be helpless, and indignant and angry like men who are betrayed. (3-4)

Wordsworth's surprises often do not, as here, produce anger or fear; frequently they are not overwhelming. But they very often do include an astonishment which is linked to an ''under-expression''—elements which seem to be at the core of Wordsworthian serendipity. For the poet insists repeatedly on a mind *fitted* for the serendipitous discovery, an under-consciousness alert to the ''under-expression''—or, in the memorable language of the 1805 *Prelude*, a mind

> that feeds upon infinity,
> That is exalted by an under-presence,
> The sense of God, or whatsoe'er is dim
> Or vast in its own being.
> (13.70-73)

Frequent in Wordsworth's poetry is a suggestion that Divine Providence, or, with equal significance, the blessing of Nature, is most readily available to the mind that is already fitted to accept them—a mind or ''a heart / That watches and receives'' (''The Tables Turned'' 31-32). This additional paradox in the circuitous paths of serendipity is a matter which Wordsworth repeatedly reaffirms: that the surprise of the serendipitous discovery often fulfills an under-conscious sense of *expectation* of the unexpected. Wordsworth's truth unsought is seldom truth utterly unpremeditated, and his shocks of surprise are often, significantly, shocks of *mild* surprise.

For example, take that exquisite pair of sonnets published in the *Poems in Two Volumes* of 1807 which record the poet's meditations on a pair of ships, or perhaps a single ship. For one of these sonnets, Wordsworth, in a letter to Lady Beaumont soon after the poems appeared in print, supplied not only an explanation of the poetic attempt but also a definition of the paradoxes of *his* kind of expectant, watchful serendipity: ''I am represented,'' he writes her about the sonnet beginning ''With Ships the sea was sprinkled far and nigh'' (*PW* 3: 18) to the reader ''as casting my eyes over the sea.'' This process is crucial for Wordsworth: the mind, in what appears to be a state of ''comparative listlessness'' which can be more accurately called, in his phrase, ''a pleasurable state of feeling with respect to the whole prospect,'' is suddenly ''all at once . . . awakened and fastened in a moment.'' And after this external impulse, this discovery, ''the mind being once fixed and rouzed, all the rest comes from itself'' (*MY*, pt. 1, May 21, 1807, 2: 148–49).

The other sonnet describes even more completely the condition of a wise passiveness so often essential to successful serendipity in Wordsworth. In this sonnet there is no discovery at all, only the impending *sense* of discovery, the anticipation of the unforeseeable, the readiness for the unexpected: ''Where lies the Land to which yon Ship must go?'' (1). More important than the question is the mood in which it is asked, a mood of mental preparedness, of ''doubt, and something dark, / Of the old Sea some reverential fear'' (*PW* 3: 18, lines 12–13). This receptive mental state is the condition generally needed to encounter the highest serendipitous epiphany in Wordsworth, and it is the condition he recommends in his letter to Lady Beaumont and to her sister, and to all his readers. Such a state of receptivity is what makes possible the promise made by the poet in the considerably later Ecclesiastical Sonnet on Emigrant French Clergy: "Chance / Opens a way for life" (*PW* 3: 402, lines 4–5).

It is, in fact, inherent in the very nature of things, and of humanity, that an expectant hope for the unexpectable, for the change which truly opens a way for life, must survive. And when such expectant hope manifests itself in any individual soul, the stage is set for serendipity, the discovery unsought but not totally unprepared for. Thus, still later, in the series of poems which grew out of Wordsworth's tour of Scotland with his daughter Dora in 1831, he writes of "the Highland Broach," a symbol for vanishing and vanished Scottish Highland glory and independence. It is a symbol now fading, he predicts, and soon to be gone:

> Soon, like a lingering star forlorn
> Among the novelties of morn,
> While young delights on old encroach,
> Will vanish the last Highland Broach.
> (*PW* 3: 273, lines 75–78)

But in the world of serendipity, no loss is necessarily permanent, no mutability wholly triumphant, no expectancy without its eventual reward:

> But when, from out their viewless bed,
> Like vapours, years have rolled and spread;

And this poor verse, and worthier lays,
Shall yield no light of love or praise;
Then, by the spade, or cleaving plough,
Or torrent from the mountain's brow,
Or whirlwind, reckless what his might
Entombs, or forces into light;
Blind Chance, a volunteer ally,
That oft befriends Antiquity,
And clears Oblivion from reproach,
May render back the Highland Broach.

(79–90)

There is no evidence but hope to support the poet's claim here, but for Wordsworth hope will suffice to bring about the needed discovery of truth unsought: "Blind Chance, a volunteer ally, / That oft befriends. . . ."

Much in the tone of these passages will have suggested Wordsworth's awareness of writing here in a great and profound literary and philosophic tradition in which Milton was also, obviously, a major participant. As usual with Wordsworth, it would be a tradition to which he would insistently apply his own fresh touches and his own distinctive views. It is unnecessary to emphasize the perfectly familiar fact that, in matters of tradition, philosophy, and theology, Wordsworth was always his own man and that whatever the growth and development of his life, even including his efforts at times to accommodate opinions and beliefs widely held around him, he remained in these matters quite independent. *Orthodoxy*, orthodoxy total and unmixed, is not a word which well characterizes Wordsworth at any of his stages of life. But he was as capable of making artistic use of orthodox doctrines as he was of departing from them when it suited him. Without, therefore, being concerned with the oft-discussed and still oft-baffling question of where and to what extent Wordsworth can be called a Christian, we can observe that the Christian doctrine of Redemption, together with its accompanying Judaic roots, embodies the quintessential act of serendipity in the universe. It is, in fact, the grandest and most universal example possible of the unexpected discovery of pure joy in the midst of a quest for other and lesser things. This redemptive discovery is exemplified in the experience of Mary Magdalene coming to the Tomb to anoint the dead body of Jesus and worrying over how she would get the stone rolled away from the entrance, only to find that there was no stone and no corpse either, only her risen Lord. That the sense of serendipity permeates Christian and Judaic theology and that serendipity from the hand of God is the constant theme of the Bible are probably perfectly evident to anyone who has given much thought to these matters. There is no need to explore the scriptural details here, especially since they have been so well explored in a thin but brilliantly rich book entitled *The Sudden in the Scripture* by biblical scholar David Daube.

But Wordsworth would not even have had to go to church, though of course he did, nor read his Bible, though of course his writing and thought are immersed in scripture, to learn of the great Christian paradox of this ultimate serendipity. If indeed he required a source beyond his own experience here, that source could have been, as for many other things, Milton alone, the Milton of *Paradise Lost* who writes of Adam's learning of serendipitous Redemption from Michael the Archangel, so that Adam, "our Sire," becomes "Replete with joy and wonder" (*PL* 12.466–67). And in the suddenness of the discovery, Adam exclaims:

O goodness infinite, goodness immense!
That all this good of evil shall produce,
And evil turn to good; more wonderful
Than that which by creation first brought forth
Light out of darkness! full of doubt I stand,
Whether I should repent me now of sin
By mee done and occasion'd, or rejoice
Much more, that much more good thereof shall
 spring,
To God more glory, more good will to Men
From God, and over wrath grace shall abound.
       (*PL* 12.469–78)

These exclamations of wonder, of rapture, of joy underline the surprise, the serendipity, of Adam's discovery of God's omnipotence, the divine ability to produce out of seemingly unpromising materials the stuff of miracles and highest aspirations, to bring on the time when losing Paradise can mean gaining much more than could have been lost—in Michael's words,

    for then the Earth
Shall all be Paradise, far happier place
Than this of Eden, and far happier days.
       (*PL* 12.463–65)

Wordsworth, constantly fascinated with the serendipity that pervades his works, would not miss this ultimate extension of the principle, this highest of all discoveries of things unlooked for. Nor, whatever his continuing concerns over the essentially separate matter of church government and theological institutions, would he have felt any aversion, or anything but profoundest reverence, for this eternal view of the basic serendipity underlying human existence. There is great power in the knowledge possessed by Milton's newly enlightened Adam who faces expulsion from Eden but who is armed now with the truth: "Greatly instructed I shall hence depart, / Greatly in peace of thought" (PL 12.557-58), he pledges, and then he enunciates that marvelous series of paradoxes which, in a sense, include all the possible kinds of serendipity, all that Wordsworth or the three Princes of Serendip could ever experience:

> Henceforth I learn, that to obey is best,
> And love with fear the only God, to walk
> As in his presence, ever to observe
> His providence, and on him sole depend,
> Merciful over all his works, with good
> Still overcoming evil, and by small
> Accomplishing great things, by things deem'd
>   weak
> Subverting worldly strong, and worldly wise
> By simply meek; that suffering for Truth's sake
> Is fortitude to highest victory,
> And to the faithful Death the Gate of Life;
> Taught this by his example whom I now
> Acknowledge my Redeemer ever blest.
>   (PL 12.561-73)

It is in this state of mind, having, as the angel says, "attain'd the sum / Of wisdom" (PL 12. 575-76) that Adam and Eve depart from Paradise. They are equipped for their future, and mankind's: "The World was all before them, where to choose / Thir place of rest, and Providence thir guide" (*PL* 12.646–47). Not just the language, impressive and important as it is, but also the mood, the realization that out of the loss of Paradise comes a far happier Paradise, is renewed for us and made present in those joyous opening lines of *The Prelude* where Wordsworth tells of his own triumph of serendipity, now emerged from frustration and seeming defeat, "escaped / From the vast city" of spiritual and mental desperation where he "long had pined" (1.6–7). The editors of the Norton edition of *The Prelude* very properly make the connection with the children of Israel escaping, also serendipitously, from their own spiritual and physical bondage, to whom Moses addressed that great reminder in chapter 13 of Exodus: "Remember this day, in which ye came out from Egypt, out of the house of bondage; for by strength of hand the Lord brought you out from this place" (Ex. 13.3). Nor is this the last allusion to the Exodus of Israel, and to this same chapter of Exodus, which unites Milton's ending of *Paradise Lost* and Wordsworth's beginning of *The Prelude*. As Adam and Eve leave Eden, "with wand'ring steps and slow" (*PL* 12.608), they have "Providence [for] thir guide" (*PL* 12.647). The people of Moses had this same divine guide, we are told: "And the Lord went before them by day in a pillar of a cloud, to lead them the way" (Ex. 3.21). Wordsworth evokes all these same images:

> What dwelling shall receive me? in what vale
> Shall be my harbour? underneath what grove
> Shall I take up my home? and what clear stream
> Shall with its murmur lull me into rest?
> The earth is all before me. With a heart
> Joyous, nor scared at its own liberty,

I look about; and should the chosen guide
Be nothing better than a wandering cloud,
I cannot miss my way, I breathe again!
(1.10–18)

And as Milton's Adam well understands, these references to Divine Guidance which conducts along unpredictable trails to an astonishing Paradise happier far are all metaphors for the Christian Redemption, that ultimate experience of universal serendipity.

It is in this context of the Redemption that Wordsworth writes the wonderful sonnet on his child Catharine, which was "suggested" by her, as he told Miss Fenwick, "long after her death" (PW 3: 423):

Surprised by joy—impatient as the Wind
I turned to share the transport—Oh! which whom
But Thee, deep buried in the silent tomb,
That spot which no vicissitude can find?
Love, faithful love, recalled thee to my mind—
But how could I forget thee? Through what power,
Even for the least division of an hour,
Have I been so beguiled as to be blind
To my most grievous loss!—That thought's return
Was the worst pang that sorrow ever bore,
Save one, one only, when I stood forlorn,
Knowing my heart's best treasure was no more;
That neither present time, nor years unborn
Could to my sight that heavenly face restore.
(PW 3: 16)

CHAPTER FOUR

"Gentle Agitations of the Mind"

"In truth, I never wrote anything with so much glee," Wordsworth recalled a half century after the composition of *The Idiot Boy* (*PW* 2: 478). A number of readers (I confess myself one) have felt much the same pleasure in reading the poem that its author claimed to have experienced in its writing. Typical of such appreciation is that expressed by a lady friend of John Wordsworth, whom the poet cites in a letter as having said that *The Idiot Boy*, which was by far the longest of Wordsworth's contributions to the original edition of *Lyrical Ballads*, was "of all the poems her delight; [she] could talk of no thing else" (*EY* 320).

But not everyone has shared this delight and glee. Robert Southey's famous and mostly obtuse critique in *Critical Review* for October 1798 dismisses *The Idiot Boy* as an "important" (198) but a failed experiment: "No tale less deserved the labour that appears to have been bestowed upon this" (200). Coleridge, at least in retrospect, in *Biographia Literaria*, found the poem contemptible: "The idiocy of the *boy* is so evenly balanced by the folly of the *mother*, as to present to the general reader rather a laughable burlesque on the blindness of anile dotage" than a truly poetic depiction of love (*BL*, ed. Shawcross 2: 35–36). The young John Wilson, one of Wordsworth's earliest and most devoted disciples, was not converted to *The Idiot Boy*, about which he wrote the poet in 1802 protesting the impropriety of the poem, for, he says, *The Idiot Boy* presents an example of the fact that "many feelings which are undoubtedly natural . . . are improper subjects for poetry" (Smith 56). Echoing such comments, but more personal in his attacks, Lord Byron made *The Idiot Boy* the focus of his treatment of Wordsworth in the *English Bards and Scotch Reviewers* of 1809, the Wordsworth who, according to Byron there,

> both by precept and example, shows
> That prose is verse, and verse is merely prose;
> Convincing all, by demonstration plain,
> Poetic souls delight in prose insane;
> And Christmas stories tortured in rhyme
> Contain the essence of the true sublime.
> Thus, when he tells the tale of Betty Foy,
> The idiot mother of 'an idiot boy;'
> A moon-struck, silly lad, who lost his way,
> And, like his bard, confounded night with day;
> So close on each pathetic part he dwells,
> And each adventure so sublimely tells,
> That all who view the 'idiot in his glory'
> Conceive the bard the hero of the story.
>
> (241–54)

And these kinds of responses are still echoed by modern critics. Karl Kroeber, a century and a half after Byron's and Coleridge's attacks on the poem, insists that "Wordsworth's idiot lacks . . . authenticity" and regrets that "the implicit horror of the boy's condition is insufficiently developed" (196, n16). In short, as Geoffrey Hartman has observed, *The Idiot Boy* has never been a really widely loved poem; in it "Wordsworth was fated to displease both the gentle reader of his day and ours" (149).

Certainly there is no reason simply to dismiss these critics
and their opinions. Some of these writers, indeed, do, though
in their own negative way, direct our attention, as we shall see,
to some of the most striking and significant features of the poem,
and in that sense they can be of value. But their main objection
to *The Idiot Boy* was probably best answered by Wordsworth
himself, long ago, in *Prelude* 13:

> There are who think that strong affections, love
> Known by whatever name, is falsely deemed
> A gift, to use a term which they would use,
> Of vulgar nature; that its growth requires
> Retirement, leisure, language purified
> By manners studied and elaborate;
> That whoso feels such passion in its strength
> Must live within the very light and air
> Of courteous usages refined by art.
>
> (186–94)

In fact, *The Idiot Boy* must be viewed and understood in the
light of the complex intentions in the poet's mind which produced it. In the Preface to *Lyrical Ballads* of 1800, Wordsworth
insists that each one of the poems in that volume ''has a purpose.'' That purpose, in general, he says, is ''to illustrate the
manner in which our feelings and ideas are associated in a state
of excitement'' (*Prose* 1: 125), and it is not difficult to apply such
a general intention to the specific instance of *The Idiot Boy*, the
one poem of all of Wordsworth's lyrical ballads of 1798 which
seems most concerned with a state of excitement and agitation
in which intellect and emotion, ''our feelings and ideas,'' are
forced together, mixed, jumbled—''are associated.'' But in that

original Preface to *Lyrical Ballads* of 1800, though the passage is omitted in versions coming after 1836, Wordsworth continues even more pointedly. His aim, he says, and here he specifies that he is talking directly about *The Idiot Boy*, is "to follow the fluxes and refluxes of the mind when agitated by the great and simple affections of our nature" (126). This poetic study of the agitated mind, the poet adds, is to be accomplished, for example, "by tracing the maternal passion through many of its more subtle windings, as in . . . the Idiot Boy" (126)—confirming the essential rightness, after all, for all its ponderous irony, of Coleridge's and Byron's suggestions that the poem's subject is much more *Betty* Foy than Johnny, or in Byron's smirking phrase, "the idiot mother of 'an idiot boy.' " All this is to be done, says Wordsworth in this same Preface, in a general context of a poetic study and depiction of "the primary laws of our nature" (122). These are impressive claims, and we shall see how well they are justified by the unique accomplishment of the poet in *The Idiot Boy*.

The letter from John Wilson already cited, in which the young Wilson praises the *Lyrical Ballads* in general but expresses his reservations concerning *The Idiot Boy*, elicited a lengthy and fascinating response from Wordsworth. In it, the poet constantly apologizes that his headache, his stomachache, his fatigue, his "habits of mind" (353) make it impossible for him to answer Wilson in the thorough detail he would prefer. Nevertheless, he takes the time to make several highly significant claims for *The Idiot Boy*.

The first of these claims is Wordsworth's admission that he intends, by many means, of course, but including the publishing of this poem, to create or develop a new audience for poetry, both an individual and a mass audience, a democratic audience—

what we might properly call a *modern* audience. The poet was later to write urgently of this challenge in *The Prelude*, where he observes of the aristocratic literary tradition holding sway during his own youth,

> How books mislead us, seeking their reward
> From judgments of the wealthy Few, who see
> By artificial lights; how they debase
> The Many for the pleasure of those Few;
> Effeminately level down the truth
> To certain general notions, for the sake
> Of being understood at once, or else
> Through want of better knowledge in the heads
> That framed them; flattering self-conceit with
>   words.
> That, while they most ambitiously set forth
> Extrinsic differences, the outward marks
> Whereby society has parted man
> From man, neglect the universal heart.
>   (13.208–20)

Similarly, in the 1802 letter to John Wilson, the poet rises to his correspondent's challenge that *The Idiot Boy* fails as a poem because "nothing is a fit subject for poetry which does not please," by arguing,

> But here follows a question, Does not please whom? Some have little knowledge of natural imagery of any kind, and, of course, little relish for it, some are disgusted with the very mention of the words pastoral poetry, sheep or shepherds,

some cannot tolerate a poem with a ghost or any supernatural agency in it, others would shrink from an animated description of the pleasures of love, as from a thing carnal and libidinous some cannot bear to see delicate and refined feelings ascribed to men in low conditions of society, because their vanity and self-love tell them that these belong only to themselves and men like themselves in dress, station, and way of life: others are disgusted with the naked language of some of the most interesting passions of men, because either it is indelicate, or gross, or [vu]lgar. . . . I return then to [the] question, please whom? or what? I answer, human nature, as it has been [and eve]r will be. But where are we to find the best measure of this? I answer, [from with]in; by stripping our own hearts naked, and by looking out of ourselves to[wards me]n who lead the simplest lives most according to nature men who [ha]ve never known false refinements, wayward and artificial desires, false criti[ci]sms, effeminate habits of thinking and feeling, or who, having known these [t]hings, have outgrown them. This latter class is the most to be depended upon, but it is very small in number. People in our rank in life are perpetually falling into one sad mistake, namely, that of supposing that human nature and the persons they associate with are one and the same thing. Whom do we generally associate with? gentlemen, persons of fortune, professional men, ladies persons who can afford to buy or can easily procure books of half a guinea price, hot-pressed, and printed upon superfine paper. These persons are, it is true, a part of human nature, but we err lamentably if we suppose them to be fair representatives of the vast mass of human existence. And yet few ever consider books but with reference to their power of pleasing these persons and men of a higher rank few descend lower among cottages and fields and among children. A man must have done this habitually before his judgment upon the Idiot Boy would be in any way decisive with me. (*EY* 354–55)

There is a transforming defiance here, certainly related to the reshaping of human nature which Wordsworth had once hoped for and supposed was being carried on in the Revolution in France ten years earlier, but the defiance would perhaps surpass in importance, especially for the world of literature, all the political and physical upheavals involving the Bastille, the guillotine, Beaupuy, or Robespierre. We are witness, in the composition and defense of *The Idiot Boy*, to the unveiling of a new and ultimately triumphant intellectual freedom, the freedom of the reading mind, of the inner integrity of unranked human nature.

In this same letter to Wilson, Wordsworth reveals too his determination to use poetry, and specifically such a poem as *The Idiot Boy*, to lead his readers into a state of purified feeling, to restore them to a harmony with their own true nature. It is the cry of the devout poet–educator, a cry for reform:

> You have given me praise for having reflected
> faithfully in my poems the feelings of human
> nature I would fain hope that I have done so. But
> a great Poet ought to do more than this he ought
> to a certain degree to rectify men's feelings, to give
> them new compositions of feeling, to render their
> feelings more sane pure and permanent, in short,
> more consonant to nature, that is, to eternal
> nature, and the great moving spirit of things. He
> ought to travel before men occasionally as well as
> at their sides. (*EY* 355)

Lord Byron's snide suggestion in *English Bards and Scotch Reviewers* that *The Idiot Boy* is somehow autobiographical, that in some sense "the bard" is "the hero of the story," is also touched on in advance in Wordsworth's letter to Wilson. There *is* true heroism, and it is partly autobiographical, the poet insists, in *The Idiot Boy*. But Johnny Foy is not the hero of the story. Rather, it is the idiot who calls forth, in a way inspires, some of the noblest heroism of which human nature is capable. The poet acknowledges "the loathing and disgust which many people have at the sight of an Idiot" (*EY* 356), but he hopes to inspire a higher response, one which he himself has experienced:

> I have indeed often looked upon the conduct
> of fathers and mothers of the lower classes of
> society towards Idiots as the great triumph of the
> human heart. It is there that we see the strength,
> disinterestedness, and grandeur of love, nor have
> I ever been able to contemplate an object that calls
> out so many excellent and virtuous sentiments

without finding it hallowed thereby and having something in me which bears down before it, like a deluge, every feeble sensation of disgust and aversion. (*EY* 357)

Finally, in this letter answering the objections raised by John Wilson to *The Idiot Boy*, Wordsworth touches on a point which was of obvious concern to him during the early period of his poetic career. This is the matter of language. The Preface to *Lyrical Ballads*, that complex statement of poetic theory and intent, makes its most powerful and perhaps its most significant claim on our attention today in its resounding calls for a simplified and realistic poetic diction, "a selection of language really used by men" (*Prose* 1: 123). In that Preface, the poet acknowledges the need for thoughtful study and discussion to determine "in what manner language and the human mind act and re-act on each other" (121). We are in *The Idiot Boy* in the presence of a poet much concerned with linguistic theory and practice, with an almost scientifically observant interest in the "plainer and more emphatic language," as he insistently calls it, of "humble and rustic life" (125). Wordsworth's findings on the language of rustic men and women, as expressed in the Preface, clearly have a great deal to do with *The Idiot Boy*. The language, especially, that is, the vocabulary, of the men of rural England, once it is "selected" and "purified," given its metrical shape, is the best language for poetry "because such men hourly communicate with the best objects from which the best part of language is originally derived" (125).

Thus, the poet advances a claim for a genuinely realistic diction in poetry, to "convey . . . feelings and notions in simple and unelaborated expressions," in a down-to-earth diction which, by comparison with the falsified language of the most widely accepted poetry of that day, offers "a more permanent, and a far more philosophical language" (125). This claim to be presenting a new kind of poetry in a new kind of poetic diction is of course much discussed and somewhat disputed. The purpose of referring to it here is to emphasize its importance to any reading of *The Idiot Boy*, for that poem, perhaps more than any other included in the 1798 *Lyrical Ballads*, is continuous in both theory and practice with the claims made in the Preface to *Lyrical Ballads*. And in his letter to John Wilson, Wordsworth notes that if Wilson has a problem with *The Idiot Boy* it is because of the "manner" in which "language and the human mind act and re-act upon each other" (Preface 121). Writes the poet, "I must content myself simply with observing that it is probable that the principle cause of your dislike to this particular poem lies in the *word* Idiot" (*EY* 357). The poet admits the difficulty: language can indeed be intractable. He acknowledges what some modern critics call "the prison house of language" (Scholes 205). He would have preferred to avoid the word *idiot*. If there were a synonym for the term which had none of its strong negative connotations, he would have used it instead—"but there is no such word" (*EY* 357). (Incidentally, it is interesting to see how Wordsworth's search for a neutral term continues to the present day, perhaps especially among professional educators, who, in the United States at least, have tortured their vocabulary-building instincts to come up with something unloaded, from *ament* to *mentally deficient* to *mentally handicapped* to *retarded* to *backward* to the currently most popular but least candid term *special*.)

But despite the occasional intractability of language, to which even the greatest of poets must sometimes acquiesce, there is still, for Wordsworth anyway, a "more permanent, and a far more philosophical" basis for poetic truth in the freshening effect of his determination to employ direct and realistic language in poetry. In such intentions for increased honesty and objectivity there is actually a moral position, a reformer's position, for a poet to take. It has required almost two centuries for literary scholars and critics to catch up with Wordsworth here. One of the best of today's critics, Robert Scholes, writes of the ways in which traditions of diction and narration and the structures of language are, and not only by unthinking or careless readers, "perceived as part of a system of psycho-social dependencies that inhibit both individual human growth and significant social change." Both of these, individual growth and significant social change, are avowed intents of Wordsworth in his poetry. "To challenge and lay bare these structures" of language and expectation, continues Scholes, "is thus a necessary prelude to any improvement in the human situation" (212). Thus it is not enough for Wordsworth merely to try to tell the truth about language or about life, important to him as those truths are. It is much more important for him to observe those truths, in even their most minute distinctions, in order to provoke the mind, his own mind and that of his reader, to mental activity. This process, involving not just humble and rustic language but even, he says, a kind of linguistic core of human experience, what he calls in *The Prelude* "the ghostly language of the ancient earth" (2.309), leads to an intellectual activity which, in a key passage on his epistemology in *Prelude* 2, the poet describes as "gentle agitations of the mind." Observe the details of the process as the poet describes it there:

> All that I beheld
> Was dear, and hence to finer influxes

The mind lay open, to a more exact
And close communication. Many are our joys
In youth, but oh! what happiness to live
When every hour brings palpable access
of knowledge, when all knowledge is delight,
And sorrow is not there! The seasons came,
And every season wheresoe'er I moved
Unfolded transitory qualities
Which, but for this most watchful power of love,
Had been neglected; left a register
Of permanent relations, else unknown.
Hence life, and change, and beauty, solitude
More active even than "best society"—
Society made sweet as solitude
By inward concords, silent, inobtrusive
And gentle agitations of the mind
From manifold distinctions, difference
Perceived in things, where, to the unwatchful
        eye,
No difference is, and hence, from the same
        source,
Sublimer joy.

(2.281–302)

This key epistemological passage has everything to do with what the poet attempts in *The Idiot Boy*, for all of us at some early stage of, usually infantile, development, pass through the condition which is more or less permanent with Johnny Foy. This is not primarily the condition of the idiot but rather of the initiate. In it, all things are new or at least seem newly discovered, and all things are wonderful. We have, for example, Johnny's delighted exclamation over what is for him a total novelty, the lonely and mysteriously transforming hours of the depths of night. There is possibly not much novel and wonderful about a shining moon and the hooting of owls for any of us *now*. To give these "things of everyday," or every night, in Coleridge's words in *Biographia Literaria*, "the charm of novelty . . . by awakening the mind's attention from the lethargy of custom" (*BL*, ed. Watson 14: 169), Wordsworth takes us into the primitive undeveloped mind of an idiot boy to remind us of the complicated responses we all must have had at one early time in our lives to the differences between night and day:

> The cocks did crow to-whoo, to-whoo,
> And the sun did shine so cold!
>
> (450–51)

The poet's moral, or social, purpose is in fact founded upon this effort to combine the novel with the commonplace. He gently agitates the mind in order to expand it. As he writes in the letter to Wilson, "[It] is not enough for me as a poet, to delineate merely such feelings as all men *do* sympathize with but, it is also highly desirable to add to these others, such as all men *may* sympathize with, and such as there is reason to believe they would be better and more moral beings if they did sympathize with" (*EY* 358).

Such a lofty aim may seem incongruous in the context of a poem of such "low" characteristics as *The Idiot Boy*. But the incongruity is intentional and is, indeed, part of a great literary tradition of conscious incongruity. Mary Jacobus convincingly and correctly identifies the place of Wordsworth's poem in that long and impressive line of "affirmative" comedy which includes, as she says, such other "saintly fools . . . in whom extreme simplicity becomes a virtue" as Lawrence Sterne's Uncle Toby and Henry Fielding's Parson Adams (255). The great ancestor of this line is, of course, Don Quixote. Cervantes tells us clearly that Don Quixote was uncomprehending, mad; his brain, we are told, dried up. But by the Romantic Age, this madman or idiot was an example of the long-ignored truths of simple nature. About Quixote, with whom he describes a visionary encounter in *The Prelude*, Wordsworth writes, in lines which might almost equally apply to Johnny Foy:

> I to him have given
> A substance, fancied him a living man,
> A gentle dweller in the desert, crazed
> By love and feeling, and internal thought
> Protracted among endless solitudes;
> Have shaped him wandering upon this quest!
> Nor have I pitied him; but rather felt
> Reverence was due to a being thus employed;
> And thought that, in the blind and awful lair
> Of such a madness, reason did lie couched.
>
> (5.143–52)

Similarly, William Hazlitt in 1819 could also be speaking of *The Idiot Boy* when he says of Cervantes' novel, "The pathos and dignity of the sentiments are often disguised under the ludicrousness of the subject; and provoke laughter when they might well draw tears" (6: 108). As Jacobus observes, the works of this tradition of affirmative comedy are "designed to disappoint the reader's expectations about narrative" (257), a design certainly central to *The Idiot Boy*. And Wordsworth's announced subject of the depths and triumphs of human love "is celebrated through comedy, not in spite of it" (259).

There are, then, in *The Idiot Boy*, so defiantly simple a poem on its surface, a number of complex strands. There is the poet's desire to agitate the reader's mind and provoke the reader's imagination by a depiction of "the great and simple affections." There is also his intention to rip out of the hands of "the wealthy Few" their longtime monopoly of books and poetry. There is, further, his desire to lead his readers into enlarged sympathies and purer moral feelings. And there is his aim to do all this in the context of the tradition of the affirmative comedy of feeling. But these multiple aims are not only complex but in some ways actually divergent. What can unify them, what the poet in this poem depends on to cement these incongruous elements, is his attention to the theory of language, an attention which is at once profoundly revolutionary in its concern for common speech but also very much a part of the long tradition of poetic concern over the sanctity of the word, a tradition which, in the century preceding *The Idiot Boy*, had included such masterpieces as Dryden's "Mac Flecknoe," Swift's *Gulliver's Travels*, Pope's *Dunciad*. Now in *The Idiot Boy*, a poem seemingly so different from those great works of English neoclassicism, Wordsworth once again focuses, in his own distinctive way, on both the divine and the human qualities of language, its basis and origin in our nature, and the effects of language on the "gentle agitations of the mind" both within the poem and within the receptive reader.

And it is important to recall the original plan for the *Lyrical Ballads*, that promised series of complementary poems setting forth, side by side, the supernatural and the natural commonplace. Coleridge says of that original plan for the collection that it was agreed that my endeavors should be directed to persons and characters supernatural, or at least romantic; yet so as to transfer from our inward nature a human interest and a semblance of truth sufficient to procure for these shadows of imagination that willing suspension of disbelief for the moment, which constitutes poetic faith. Mr. Wordsworth, on the other hand, was to propose to himself as his object to give the charm of novelty to things of every day, and to excite a feeling analogous to the supernatural, by awakening the mind's attention from the lethargy of custom and directing it to the loveliness and the wonders of the world before us. (*BL*, ed. Watson 14: 168–69)

Again concerning the original plan for the *Lyrical Ballads*, Coleridge writes in May of 1798 to Joseph Cottle, the intended publisher, "We deem that the volumes offered to you are to a certain degree *one work*, in *kind tho' not in degree*, as an Ode is one work—& that our different poems are as stanzas, good relatively rather than absolutely" (STC Letters 1: 412).

Though the original plan for *Lyrical Ballads* was not fulfilled, for Coleridge could not keep up with what he calls "Mr. Wordsworth's industry" (*BL* 14: 169), there are important traces of that plan still visible in the poems. In recalling near the end of *The Prelude* the early association with Coleridge, Wordsworth writes:

> Rueful woes
> Didst utter of the Lady Christabel
> And I, associate with such labor, steeped

In soft forgetfulness the livelong hours,
Murmuring of him who, joyous hap, was found,
After the perils of his moonlight ride,
Near the loud waterfall.

(14.400–06)

Particularly in *The Idiot Boy* and *Christabel* we can see most fully worked out the complementarity which lies at the heart of that original plan for the *Lyrical Ballads*. Even when the plan was finally abandoned and *Christabel* was actually omitted from the published volume, the shadow of the original intention as it appears in these two stanzaic pieces remains another fascinating basis for insight into the poetic achievement of Wordsworth, and also Coleridge, in 1798. Much of the genuine poetic power of *The Idiot Boy*, as also with much of the power of *Christabel*, lies in the relationship of the two works. Coleridge's statement that they are "good relatively rather than absolutely" may overstate the case, for the poems both seem very good on their own. But it is hard to disagree with his essential point that their interrelationship makes the two poems particularly valuable in tandem, and it is concerning that tandem relationship that the following few suggestions are made.

The numerous mistaken utterances in *Christabel* are clearly at the heart of that poem: Geraldine's polite but incautious echoing of Christabel's wish for her mother—"O mother dear! that thou wert here! / I would, said Geraldine, she were!"—which requires correction in "altered voice" (202–04); the touch of Geraldine's bosom which "worketh a spell, / Which is lord of thy utterance, Christabel!" (267–68); Bard Bracy's vow to perform that awesome form of utterance, a poetic exorcism, left tragically unfulfilled; the Baron's "half-listening" (565) misunderstanding of Bracy's vision, which leads to his confused and unperformable promise to Geraldine—"With arms more strong than harp or song, / Thy sire and I will crush the snake!" (570–71). The conclusion to *Christabel*, in the form in which Coleridge left it to us, is an ironically light-hearted discussion of this theme of the confusion of the word:

> Perhaps 'tis pretty to force together
> Thoughts so all unlike each other;
> To mutter and mock a broken charm,
> To dally with wrong that does no harm.
> Perhaps 'tis tender too and pretty
> At each wild word to feel within
> A sweet recoil of love and pity.
> And what, if in a world of sin
> (O sorrow and shame should this be true!)
> Such giddiness of heart and brain
> Comes seldom save from rage and pain,
> So talks as it's most used to do.
>
> (666–77)

If *The Idiot Boy* is a true companion piece to *Christabel*, it must have the theme of language at its core too. Wordsworth told Isabella Fenwick that "the foundation of the whole" poem is Johnny Foy's language, his summation at the end of his night's adventures of the cocks crowing with the voices of owls and the sun shining coldly in the moon's sphere. This seeming misuse of language, because it is a tale told by an idiot, qualifies as one of the "things of every day" that Coleridge said that Wordsworth proposed to make, through the transforming poetic imagination, "analogous to the supernatural." And out of this apparent misutterance grew the whole poem, "composed in the groves of Alfoxden, almost extempore" (*PW* 2: 478).

Abuse of language, in much more serious ways than Johnny Foy's ignorant, and arguably poetic, misspeaking, even extending at moments, as in *Christabel*, to aphasia, the silencing of language, occurs throughout *The Idiot Boy*. But Wordsworth keeps the tone, even amid constant peril and potential tragedy, much lighter than in Coleridge's poem; the hellishness of *Christabel* receives only a vaguely troubling echo in *The Idiot Boy*. When we first meet Old Susan Gale, we see her in a detachment of conscious mind and vocal chords that becomes typical of every character in this poem. At the beginning of the narrative she "makes a piteous moan / As if her very life would fail" (19-20), but when she stops long enough to think a bit and gain control over her utterance, "Her body—it grew better" (416). The doctor to whom Johnny's mother belatedly applies for help responds only with his own sleepy but educated kind of misutterance, an ill-suited irony that leaves us in doubt as well about his stand on Hippocrates' Oath:

> "The devil take his wisdom!" said
> The Doctor, looking somewhat grim,
> "What, Woman! should I know of him?"
> And, grumbling, he went back to bed!
> (258-61)

Even the narrator of the poem becomes tongue-tied, a non-narrator, at a loss to finish his story. Among all the possible adventures which may have befallen Johnny on his moonlight ride, the narrator can pin down nothing. He wants to, of course; it would be "a most delightful tale" (316), but the Muses themselves have been struck dumb:

I to the Muses have been bound
These fourteen years, by strong indentures.
O gentle Muses! let me tell
But half of what to him befell;
He surely met with strange adventures.

(337-41)

But the goddesses of inspired poetic utterance are silent. The Word is stilled:

O gentle Muses! is this kind?
Why will ye thus my suit repel?
Why of your further aid bereave me?
And can ye thus unfriended leave me,
Ye Muses! whom I love so well?

(342-46)

Wordsworth supplies no reason for the aphasia of both Muses and narrator at this moment of crisis. There is no evil decision or act, no Geraldine here to put a spell on tongues. Clearly the poet is in this section of the poem less concerned with the causes of this condition than with the calamitous stilling of the Word itself and the effects of that stilling, silence, the rupture of the strong indentures between divine source and poetic utterance. Clearly too he is unwilling here where he speaks of the poet's responsibility to falsify the deep nature of language for the mere delight of forcing a tale. The deconstructionist critics of today rightly express concern that by the forcing of narration, the illusion of sequence, and by the violation of integrity in language, many of us, both readers and poets, "give a spurious order to chaos, creating selves and worlds both bounded by language" (Scholes 207). The narrator of *The Idiot Boy*—I refer of course to

Wordsworth's persona, not to Wordsworth himself—or at least his sternly silent Muses, can refuse to fall into this pervasive error. The poem now becomes an antinarrative.

Wordsworth underscores the linguistic danger even more impressively in his treatment of another character in the poem. For in the depiction of Betty Foy above all the other misusers of language or victims of the unutterable in *The Idiot Boy*, the poet revealingly traces some basic laws of our nature, traces in fact the causes and effects of the mother's misutterance. Much of the poem consists of a report of Betty's words and comments on her use of language. At the beginning, as she instructs her son, she is perfectly composed and clear:

> And Betty o'er and o'er has told
> The Boy, who is her best delight,
> Both what to follow, what to shun,
> What do, and what to leave undone,
> How turn to left, and how to right.
>
> (52–56)

But as the night wears on and Old Susan Gale's condition seems to deteriorate, and Johnny does not return with the doctor, Betty Foy falls victim to a literally dumbfounding anxiety, the anxiety of separation from her physically mature but mentally infantile son, her Idiot Boy. Wordsworth, by giving her such a son, makes Betty Foy, in effect, a perpetually nursing mother, one whose motherhood leaves her always in that kind of state of excitement which the poet promises to observe with particular attention. The poet is faithful to his objective of tracing the primary laws of human nature in selecting as his heroine such a mother of such a son. In a state of excitement we may quickly reach a point at which we cannot associate ideas at all, as Coleridge's lines on how "'tis pretty to force together / Thoughts" suggest. For Betty Foy, that point always lies nearby, a fact she lives with but is unable to overcome, because the infantile mentality of her son does not go away. For her it is that son's becoming lost which provokes the anxiety resulting in her own infantile behavior and utterance, but for all of us, as for the once seemingly well-adjusted Christabel and her father, for whom the crisis presented by Geraldine is beyond coping, there may be similar limits past which our minds and our voices cannot securely go. The combination within the poem of overwhelming and conflicting anxieties and excitations results in a severe instance of the breakdown of language in Betty Foy. She is first depicted as one "bent on her intent" (17), totally capable in her use of language and appreciative of its correct use in others. But the intensifying anxiety of the night's adventures reduces her to raving: "Unworthy things she talked, and wild" (239). She attacks the innocent Pony, the ignorant doctor, the sickly Susan, the Idiot Johnny—all in her "sad distemper" (238). Eventually the slammed door of the doctor reduces her to speechless fear and to thoughts of suicide.

In *Christabel*, in the form we have it, the failure of the Word is permanent; Geraldine's utterance-dominating spell totally triumphs over both father and daughter. By contrast, it is a typically Wordsworthian cure for essentially the same "sad distemper" that *The Idiot Boy* presents. When Betty Foy forsakes suicide and self-pity, when she puts her faith back in Nature where it properly belongs (especially as represented within the poem by "the Pony . . . mild and good" [303]), her meditations lead her to the waterfall, to the Pony, and to the lost Johnny. And once she recovers from the "drunken pleasure" (380) of finding her son, Betty's power of speech returns fully and clearly, with, in fact, a clarity and accuracy which throw into strong relief Johnny's own use of language, whether we call it poetic or idiotic, his summary of the night, his confusing of cock and owl and of sun and moon, with which the poem ends—and with which, by Wordsworth's account, its composition began.

When Lord Byron dismisses *The Idiot Boy* as one of Wordsworth's "Christmas stories tortured into rhyme," he is missing, or (more likely) pretending to miss, these depths and complexities of Wordsworth's interest and experimenting in language and its relationships as both a cause and an effect of human nature. The simplicity on the surface of the poem could, and probably does, lull many a careless reader into missing a great deal of what the poet is up to.

There is, though, the further danger, beyond carelessness, of habit and custom, and these have surely affected many readers' responses to *The Idiot Boy*. In his Advertisement published with the *Lyrical Ballads* in 1798, Wordsworth admits some concern over the deadening influence of any Literary Establishment and "that most dreadful enemy to our pleasures, our own preestablished codes of decision" (*Prose* 1: 116). And in the 1800 Preface he tells us he is thinking about his poetry and his poetic theories in terms of "revolutions, not of literature alone, but likewise of society itself" (121). Perhaps the chief quality of *The Idiot Boy*, finally, which produces in the reader "gentle," or even not so gentle, "agitations of the mind" is not its simplicity nor its "lowness" but its subversiveness. F. W. Bateson rightly observes that the poem is, in its principal effects on the reader, "not merely outside the literary tradition" but "written in a deliberate defiance of it" (200). Nor is this defiantly revolutionary quality only an artistic stance assumed by the poet.

"The gross, offensive non-literariness is," says Bateson, "an important part of [the poem's] meaning" (200). It is Wordsworth's technique, then, nowhere else more fully attempted or achieved than in *The Idiot Boy*, to provoke us as readers, to agitate the mind in order to shape it, to educate it, to reform it, and at the same time, in an intimately connected aim, to vivify and purify our use of language and our attentiveness to its demands. As he says in the Preface:

> For our continued influxes of feeling are modified and directed by our thoughts, which are indeed the representatives of all our past feelings; and, as by contemplating the relation of these general representatives to each other, we discover what is really important to men, so, by the repetition and continuance of this act, our feelings will be connected with important subjects, till at length, if we be originally possessed of much sensibility, such habits of mind will be produced, that, by obeying blindly and mechanically the impulses of those habits, we shall describe objects, and utter sentiments, of such a nature, and in such connection with each other, that the understanding of the Reader must necessarily be in some degree enlightened, and his affections strengthened and purified. (127)

These are high aspirations—to produce sensitivity of mind, enlightenment of understanding, purifying of affections, and all based on the truthfulness and realism of utterance, of language. The function of the poet and his poetic tools, it has been well said, is to participate in "the perpetual motion of . . . language. In this function they keep language open to life" (Scholes 209). Lord Byron's facetious charge that Wordsworth in *The Idiot Boy* claimed to achieve "the essence of the true sublime" contains an ironic truth beyond Byron's intent in the remark but not beyond the profound significance of Wordsworth's poem itself. For under the spell of the poet's vision and the refining power of his language, under the "gentle agitations of the mind," we are brought to a condition in the relationship between poem and reader which resembles that of the young child in Nature, when, as Wordsworth promises in *The Prelude*, "every hour brings palpable access / Of knowledge" (2.286–87).

CHAPTER FIVE

To Enlarge the Circle of Sensibilities: "The Mystery of Words"

There may be no more demanding poet than Wordsworth. The demands he makes, though, are not those of other poets. He does not perplex by an unfamiliar vocabulary nor a complexly involved syntax nor by learned allusions and literary citations in a variety of often very exotic tongues requiring explanatory footnotes exceeding in the space they occupy the poetry they are designed to elucidate. (I am thinking here of so great a poet as T. S. Eliot and so great a poem as Eliot's *The Waste Land,* of which, when it was written, the intended publisher complained that it was too short to be published as a separate book. So to lengthen it, Eliot obligingly added a series of footnotes which essentially doubled the length of the poem but which sometimes only deepened the mystery; the result is that some modern printings of *The Waste Land* have further editorial footnotes to explain the footnotes.)

That is not Wordsworth's way. But *in* his way, he is no less demanding a poet than Eliot or other still more difficult writers. Wordsworth's difficulty, however, is not linguistic or stylistic. One of the hardest things about him is that he does not seem hard at all in some of his most demanding spots. Where other poets can seem to immerse the reader in difficulties, Wordsworth aims, as he says in the 1800 Preface to *Lyrical Ballads,* at conveying to his reader "the sense of difficulty overcome," a sense, however, as he acknowledges, only admissable "if his Reader's mind be sound and vigorous" (*Prose* 1: 150).

Perhaps there is no better example of these multiple paradoxes of complexity in seeming simplicity, of demands so deep but so easy to pass by, than the wonderful poem "Lucy Gray."

> Oft I had heard of Lucy Gray:
> And, when I crossed the wild,
> I chanced to see at break of day
> The solitary child.
>
> No mate, no comrade Lucy knew;
> She dwelt on a wide moor,
> —The sweetest thing that ever grew
> Beside a human door!
>
> (1–8)

Anyone who has ever lost a child, in any sense, will recognize one of the great demands Wordsworth makes on his readers here. A child lost to death, or just to opposition, a child lost forever or only for a moment, is so painful a topic, so inviting to panic and terror in its uncertainty, as almost to seem unfit for poetry; indeed, it *is* a subject unfit for the poetry of most poets.

Uncertainty. *That* is the chief and most painful demand which Wordsworth makes upon his readers. And in this he differs astonishingly from his predecessors among English poets who had dealt with tales of lost children. One of these poets, specifically cited by Wordsworth in his note on "Lucy Gray" that he dictated to Isabella Fenwick nearly half a century after the poem's composition, is George Crabbe. Wordsworth says that he intended to contrast with Crabbe. In "Lucy Gray," he tells us, "the way in which the incident was treated and spiritualizing of the character might furnish hints for contrasting the imaginative influences which I have endeavoured to throw over common life with Crabbe's matter of fact style of treating subject of the same kind." But, he adds, "This is not spoken to [Crabbe's] disparagement, far from it; but to direct the attention of thoughtful readers . . . to a comparison that may both enlarge the circle of their sensibilities, and tend to produce in them a catholic judgment" (*PW* 1: 360). This is a typical aim of the poet's efforts at education through poetry.

Wordsworth cites no specific work of Crabbe's, but he must have had in mind such a poem as Crabbe's "Sir Eustace Grey"—note the similarity of family names with "Lucy Gray." In that work, Crabbe has his Sir Eustace tell about the loss of his innocent little son and daughter, "two cherub-things . . . , / A gracious girl, a glorious boy" (84–85). Just as Wordsworth's little Lucy Gray was "The sweetest thing that ever grew / Beside a human door" (7–8), Sir Eustace's children were flower-like too; but there the similarities cease, for Crabbe does indeed tell their story, as Wordsworth claims, in a "matter of fact style": "In youth! health! joy! in beauty's pride! / They droop'd—as flowers when blighted bow; / The dire infection came:—they died" (140–42). There is both an abruptness and a certainty here which are totally missing, because totally avoided, in Wordsworth.

Another poet writing on this theme of lost children was, of course, Wordsworth's great contemporary, the then largely ignored William Blake. Among Blake's *Songs of Innocence*, published eleven years before "Lucy Gray," are the pair of poems entitled "The Little Boy Lost" and "The Little Boy Found," in which Blake tells of a child lost in darkness—

but God ever nigh,
Appeared like his father in white.

He kissed the child & by the hand led
And to his mother brought,
Who in sorrow pale, thro' the lonely dale
Her little boy weeping sought.

("Found" 2–8)

Five years later, Blake published the *Songs of Experience*, intended
to have a complementary relationship with the earlier volume,
including a pair of poems entitled "The Little Girl Lost" and
"The Little Girl Found." This little girl is named Lyca, and she
becomes the object of a parental search which sounds very much
like Lucy Grey's:

All the night in woe
Lyca's parents go:
Over vallies deep,
While the desarts weep.

Tired and woe-begone,
Hoarse with making moan:
Arm in arm seven days,
They traced the desart ways.

("Found" 1–8)

But Lyca's parents are granted a vision which leads them out
of torment and uncertainty to a successful conclusion:

Then they followed,
Where the vision led;
And saw their sleeping child.

(45–47)

Nobody, surely, would ever accuse Blake of having a "matter of fact style," but it is crucial to observe that in telling a finished tale, one which concludes in certainty, Blake is here much closer in spirit to Crabbe than to Wordsworth.

For Wordsworth was insistent on doing something new. He was, however, thoroughly aware of this tradition of English poems dealing with lost children; indeed he evokes it intentionally. In the 1800 Preface to *Lyrical Ballads*, that same year and volume in which "Lucy Gray" was first published, Wordsworth quotes as "one of the most justly admired stanzas" in the anonymous and popular poem "Babes in the Wood" these lines:

> These pretty Babes with hand in hand
> Went wandering up and down;
> But never more they saw the Man
> Approaching from the town.
>
> *(Prose* 1: 154)

And in lines which are surely an intentional echo of these, Wordsworth tells us of Lucy Gray,

> She wandered up and down;
> And many a hill did Lucy climb:
> But never reached the town.
>
> (30–32)

But though Wordsworth admired "Babes in the Wood" and thus was willing to echo it, he did not want to imitate it. He was doing something very different, and for 1800 certainly quite new in narrative art. He was not story-telling, not concluding, but provoking, *un-telling*, plunging his readers into a perhaps painful but also beneficial uncertainty, beneficial because it provokes mental and emotional and spiritual activity and searching. There is *no* uncertainty about the Babes in the Woods:

> Thus wandered those two prettye babes,
> Till death did end their grief;
> In one another's armes they dyed,
> As babes wanting relief.
>
> (*Caldecott* 121–24)

In contrast to these kinds of poems of narrative certainty about lost children written by Crabbe and Blake and others before Wordsworth, the poet of "Lucy Gray" seems downright addicted to ambiguity and confusion. And there is a lot more, and something quite different, in Wordsworth's practice along these lines than just a somewhat sentimental, and dishonest, attempt to evade the pain of loss by refusing to acknowledge the certainty of the loss. That is assuredly not Wordsworth's way. There are numerous poems in his writing (one thinks, for example, of "The Thorn," *The Idiot Boy*, "Anecdote for Fathers," "Two April Mornings," and several spots in *The Prelude*) which have at their very core this intentional ambiguity and uncertainty, but none better than "Lucy Gray." It is an intention central to his poetic practice and theory, for, as he says in the Preface to *Lyrical Ballads*, which it seems fair to read in a special way as very much a preface to "Lucy Gray," he wanted to heal the mind of his reader from "a craving for extraordinary incident," from a lust for "frantic novels, sickly and stupid German Tragedies, and deluges of idle and extravagant stories in verse" that by his own day had seemingly become a "degrading thirst after outrageous stimulation" that would "blunt the discriminating powers of the mind, and unfitting it for all voluntary exertion . . . reduce it to a state of almost savage torpor'' (*Prose* 1: 128–30).

Consider, for example, the implications of this contrasting aim, as Wordsworth expresses it in *Prelude* 5; he is speaking of *his* kind of reader:

> He, who in his youth
> A daily wanderer among woods and fields
> With living Nature hath been intimate,
> Not only in that raw unpractised time
> Is stirred to extasy, as others are,
> By glittering verse; but further, doth receive,
> In measure only dealt out to himself,
> Knowledge and increase of enduring joy
> From the great Nature that exists in works
> Of mighty Poets. Visionary power
> Attends the motions of the viewless winds,
> Embodied in the mystery of words:
> There, darkness makes abode, and all the host
> Of shadowy things work endless changes there.
>
> (1850 5.586–99)

What an intention, and what a claim this is! Wordsworth asserts that poetry can make available something he calls "Knowledge," though quite different from the accumulations of facts and information that most people mean when they speak of knowledge. Wordsworth's kind of knowledge is very personal, very individual, "In measure only dealt out to himself." It has something to do with "visionary power." It is conveyed or provoked invisibly, perhaps unconsciously, like "the motions of the viewless winds." This Wordsworthian Knowledge comes "Embodied in the mystery of words." It is not a matter of filling the mind with facts but rather of moving the mind to activity, for it comes not in light but in darkness—"and all the host / Of shadowy things work endless changes there."

It is worthwhile, then, to take another look at "Lucy Gray" and collect observations of what is known and not known about her story—to observe *what* "Knowledge" is there "Embodied in the mystery of words." The poem, Wordsworth later told Miss Fenwick, was based on a true story told him by his sister Dorothy, "of a little girl, who not far from Halifax in Yorkshire, was bewildered in a snowstorm" and whose body was later found in a canal (*PW* 1: 360). Lucy Gray, like this factual predecessor, also gets lost in a snowstorm, but her body is not found. Indeed, whether she even died is not certain. Her parents search for her throughout the night, but instead of certainty they find only bafflement:

> The wretched parents all that night
> Went shouting far and wide;
> But there was neither sound nor sight
> To serve them for a guide.
>
> At day-break on a hill they stood
> That overlooked the moor;
> And thence they saw the bridge of wood,
> A furlong from their door.
>
> They wept—and turning homeward, cried,
> "In heaven we all shall meet;"

—When in the snow the mother spied
The print of Lucy's feet.

Then downwards from the steep hill's edge
They tracked the footmarks small;
And through the broken hawthorn hedge,
And by the long stone-wall;

And then an open field they crossed:
The marks were still the same;
They tracked them on, nor ever lost;
And to the bridge they came.

And followed from the snowy bank
Those footmarks, one by one,
Into the middle of the plank;
And further there were none!

—Yet some maintain that to this day
She is a living child;
That you may see sweet Lucy Gray
Upon the lonesome wild.

(33–60)

What a strange confusion of evidence this is! The raging snowstorm not only swallows up the little girl, it swallows all evidence of her fate: "there was neither sight nor sound." Such is, in reality, the pitiless behavior of snowstorms. But then by the light of dawn "in the snow the mother spied / The print of Lucy's feet." What kind of storm is this? What sort of snow first obliterates all sight of the little girl, then hours later reveals her footprints? They are clear footprints, too, looking as if they had been made *after* the blizzard instead of during it. The search party follows them eagerly and easily down the hill and through the hedge and along the wall and across the field, right to the middle of the bridge. But can footprints coming like these out of nowhere lead anywhere?

In truth, even before she gets lost in the storm, little Lucy Gray seems somehow "embodied in the mystery of words." Her father sends her to bring her mother back from town. How long a journey is that? Well, not far. Says Lucy, "The minster-clock has just struck two," so she lives within hearing distance of the church bells. There is also an inattention bordering on criminal neglect in all this—the supposition that it is somehow more appropriate for the little girl to go *to town* alone than for her mother to *come home* alone. But notice that the mother does come home alone, without any apparent difficulty. The poem never tells how she got there, or whether she actually waited for her daughter to arrive with the lantern, but as soon as Lucy's absence becomes apparent the mother is right there by the husband's side, joining in the search. This inattention seems almost captured in its dreadful essence by the strikingly inept simile of these lines on Lucy: "Her feet disperse the powdery snow / That rises up like smoke" (27–28), for anyone who gives the slightest thought to snow realizes that in what matters most about this snow, namely its deadly coldness, it is not at all like smoke. The inept simile is not, then, the poet's mistake (we rarely find Wordsworth making such mistakes) but rather the sign of the casual inattention by all the characters in the poem to the truth about snow, and Nature.

And yet what possible credence can an intelligent reader be expected to give to the common folklore that persists in claiming that "you may yet see sweet Lucy Gray / Upon the lonesome wild"? Sophisticated readers of great poetry at least know the truth about such naive ghostlore and rustic citings of supernatural beings. The poem tells us in clarity: "The sweet face of Lucy Gray / Will never more be seen" (11–12). And that settles the matter, of course.

But then, what to make of that astounding first stanza, that testimony of the narrator of the poem, who tells us, "I chanced to see at break of day / The solitary child"? Here is a piece of local gossip not easy to dismiss, for if we cannot trust the narrator, we have no place anywhere in the poem to place our confidence—and, as the poet warns in those lines in *The Prelude*, "all the host / Of shadowy things work endless changes there."

There is, of course, another reading for all this, a sense in which Lucy Gray may in fact be at once a mortal victim of the storms of Nature and still, in a different way, continue to be a living child, the sense in which a Child is invariably father of every Man, mother of every Woman, and continues to exist in the adult personality. But continues with considerable loss. For regardless of what readers, or Wordsworth himself, may believe about the immortality of the soul and the eternal nature of Man, there is not, except in this sense, any real *permanence* in *childhood*. We all may live forever; indeed, many believe we will. But, except in this very limited sense, the child that every adult once was is gone forever. Childhood, is, for all beholders and participants, a temporary and transitory state. All children, one way or another, are like Lucy Gray in that they can never reach the town. One cannot be an adult who arrives at the great destinations of human existence and remain thoroughly a child too.

The tension between the *bliss* of childhood and the *transitoriness* of childhood is a constant awareness in Wordsworth. And the poet repeatedly attempts what he repeatedly acknowledges to be vain attempts to perpetuate the bliss of childhood, like Goethe's Faust bidding the hastening moment to stay awhile because it is so fair—"*Verweile Doch! du bist so schön!*" There are, for example, those lines addressed by Wordsworth to the child in his Intimations of Immortality Ode, lines of which Coleridge strongly disapproved but which anyway give the essential Wordsworthian position on this matter:

> Thou, whose exterior semblance doth belie
>   Thy Soul's immensity;
> Thou best Philosopher, who yet dost keep
> Thy heritage, thou Eye among the blind,
> That, deaf and silent, read'st the eternal deep,
> Haunted for ever by the eternal mind,—
>   Mighty Prophet! Seer blest!
>   On whom those truths do rest,
> Which we are toiling all our lives to find,
> In darkness lost, the darkness of the grave,
> Thou, over whom thy Immortality
> Broods like the Day, a Master o'er a Slave,
> A Presence which is not to be put by;
> Thou, little Child, yet glorious in the might
> Of heaven-born freedom on thy being's height,
> Why with such earnest pains dost thou provoke
> The years to bring the inevitable yoke,
> Thus blindly with thy blessedness at strife?
> Full soon thy Soul shall have her earthly
>   freight,
> And custom lie upon thee with a weight,
> Heavy as frost, and deep almost as life!

(109–29)

Perhaps Lucy Gray's body, too, lies not in a snowdrift nor in the icy current of the frozen stream but, like every child eventually, buried in a grave of custom lying upon her "with a weight / Heavy as frost, and deep almost as life!"

Much the same awareness of the contrast between the constant visionary blessedness of childhood and the only occasional glimpses of insight which adults experience appears in the great sonnet of Wordsworth to his French daughter Caroline on the occasion of what was very likely their first meeting, on a beach near Calais in 1802. As the father beholds in the sunset a vision of eternity, the child scampers up and down the sand, chasing crabs and beating back waves and staying determinedly oblivious to the magnificence of Nature and the universe. And yet, the poet realizes, the little girl is, in her unconscious way, his spiritual superior:

> It is beauteous evening, calm and free,
> The holy time is quiet as a Nun
> Breathless with adoration; the broad sun
> Is sinking down in its tranquility;
> The gentleness of heaven broods o'er the Sea:
> Listen! the mighty Being is awake,
> And doth with his eternal motion make
> A sound like thunder—everlastingly.
> Dear Child! dear Girl! that walkest with me here,
> If thou appear untouched by solemn thought,
> Thy nature is not therefore less divine:
> Thou liest in Abraham's bosom all the year;
> And worshipp'st at the Temple's inner shrine,
> God being with thee when we know it not.

> (PW 3: 17)

The Intimations Ode, the sonnet to Caroline on the beach on that "beauteous evening, calm and free," and "Lucy Gray" are all pieces of a complex puzzle in which the poet seems to be gradually discovering for himself and then revealing for us his thoughts on childhood, and his understanding of the growing mind. That he considered them all pieces of the same project is attested to in his letter to Coleridge of 5 May 1809. This was the period when Wordsworth was hastening his great tract on the Convention of Cintra into publication and Coleridge at the same time was trying to arrange for the printing of his periodical *The Friend*. It is an amazing letter, full of Wordsworth's current concern that he might be prosecuted for libel for his attack in the Cintra tract on Sir Arthur Wellesley, soon to become the Duke of Wellington. It is full too of outrage and contempt for the puny minds of military men and government ministers, for, writes the poet, "Politicians . . . only look at things in the gross; the spirit always escapes their notice" (*MY* 1: 333–34). And then, abruptly in the next paragraph of the letter, Wordsworth outlines for Coleridge an intention to arrange his poems by themes in future publication. But the transition is not so abrupt as it first seems, for Wordsworth's arrangement, which he finally did adopt in 1815 according to the general outline he gives Coleridge in the 1809 letter, seems to have been designed to help "the mass of mankind," as he says, avoid this temptation to look at things in the gross while missing the spirit.

In this attempt, then, to educate and articulate the reader's sensibilities, Wordsworth chooses as the first category in the arrangement of his poems what he calls in this letter to Coleridge "Poems relating to childhood, and such feelings as rise in the mind in after life in direct contemplation of that state" (*MY* 1: 334). Within this classification the poems would not be arranged chronologically or in order of composition but with a sense of imaginative progression, beginning, he says, "with the simplest dawn of the affections or faculties and then ascending" in a gradual scale of imagination, "finally to conclude with the grand ode," "Lucy Gray" being specifically mentioned by the poet as a step along the way (MY 1: 334). There is an integrity in such an arrangement, a progressive sensitizing of the reader's mind, a sensitizing which is essential to full appreciation of the poems and which can only be ignored to our loss.

Among the specific links which bring together these puzzle pieces of childhood and the adult reflections on childhood are what Wordsworth calls "two recollections." This idea is presented in another of his letters, this one to Catherine Clarkson in January 1815. The "two recollections of childhood," which the poet there calls fundamental to his treatment of the theme, are "one that of a splendour in the objects of sense," which, now in adulthood, "is passed away, and the other an indisposition to bend to the law of death as applying to our own particular case" (MY 2: 189). "An indisposition to bend to the law of death"—here surely is a phrase that goes to the heart of the mystery and uncertainty of "Lucy Gray." The little girl *must* be dead. All our adult reasoning tells us she could not have survived the storm, or if she by some near miracle did so she would surely have returned home after her ordeal—not simply vanish into the landscape to be seen from time to time in after years. Her parents, even in their great distress, acknowledge that her earthly life has ended, for they, "turning homeward, cried, / 'In heaven we all shall meet.' " But that "indisposition to bend to the law of death" appears in the folklore of the poem, where "some maintain that to this day / She is a living child."

Another of the poems that Wordsworth told Coleridge he intended to fit into his arrangement concerning childhood and the adult contemplation of childhood is his lines addressed to Coleridge's son Hartley at the age of six, now entitled "To H.C." Once again, in these lines Wordsworth expresses an ambiguity, an uncertainty, and an "indisposition to bend" to death or other harsh realities of adult life. In these lines, written in the same year as his marriage to Mary Hutchinson and of course before they had any children of their own, Wordsworth speaks in a fatherly protective tone to the little boy whom he loved and who so frequently taught him about the perspective of children. But the main idea of this poem is not the glory of childhood but its transcience. And here there is not even the pious comfort offered by Lucy Gray's parents—"in heaven we all shall meet." For what here is so temporary, so fleeting, is not Hartley Coleridge but childhood itself. And once it is gone we shall not meet that lost childhood even in heaven. It is eternally gone. So precious, so pure, "so exquisitely wild"—and yet so transitory and with no hope for any future in itself. The poem deserves closer attention than it has generally received:

To H. C.

Six Years Old

O thou! whose fancies from afar are brought:
Who of thy words dost make a mock apparel,
And fittest to unutterable thought
The breeze-like motion and the self-born carol;
Thou faery voyager! that dost float
In such clear water, that thy boat
May rather seem
To brood on air than on an earthly stream;

Suspended in a stream as clear as sky,
Where earth and heaven do make one imagery;
O blessed vision! happy child!
Thou art so exquisitely wild,
I think of thee with many fears
For what may be thy lot in future years.

I thought of times when Pain might be thy guest,
Lord of thy house and hospitality;
And Grief, uneasy lover! never rest
But when she sate within the touch of thee.
O too industrious folly!
O vain and causeless melancholy!
Nature will either end thee quite;
Or, lengthening out thy season of delight,
Preserve for thee, by individual right,
A young lamb's heat among the full-grown flocks.
What hast thou to do with sorrow,
Or the injuries of tomorrow?
Thou art a dew-drop, which the morn brings
    forth,
Ill fitted to sustain unkindly shocks,
Or to be trailed along the soiling earth;
A gem that glitters while it lives,
And no forewarning gives;
But, at the touch of wrong, without a strife
Slips in a moment out of life.

(*PW* 1: 247)

In all this there is a kind of Shakespearean resolve "To love
that well, which thou must leave ere long" (Sonnet 73). But

much more is the poet's puzzlement over how it can be that a divinely ordered universe which takes care to make life joyous and permanent could leave so precious and pure a state as human childhood *impermanent*. Here we come up against the overwhelming loss in "Lucy Gray." The little girl was "The sweetest thing that ever grew / Beside a human door," but it is that very sweetness which "Will never more be seen" (7–8, 12).

In the abstract, all this grieving over the loss of childhood, the loss of what the very nature of human existence makes universal and inevitable, may seem, as Wordsworth says in another context, "going far to seek disquietude" (*Prelude* 5.53). But the poet cannot leave it in the abstract. Here he reminds us of Gerard Manley Hopkins's little poem entitled "Spring and Fall: To a Young Child," in which the poet tries to reason with a little girl named Margaret as she grieves for the falling of the autumn leaves from the trees, only to realize that such grieving is innate to the human spirit, child or adult, a grieving over the recognition of the limits of our earthly human nature; says Hopkins, "It is the blight man was born for, / It is Margaret you mourn for" (14–15).

Similarly, it is Wordsworth, the child Wordsworth, lost forever, whom Wordsworth the mature poet frequently grieves for in his poetry on childhood. And while he grieves this loss of part of his own person, the boy he was, he inevitably contemplates the growth of the human mind—the education which growing up provides. That little boy lost he celebrates joyously in *The Prelude*:

> Oh, many a time have I, a five year's child,
> In a small mill-race severed from his stream,
> Made one long bathing of a summer's day;

Basked in the sun, and plunged and basked again
Alternate, all a summer's day, or scoured
The sandy fields, leaping through flowery groves
Of yellow ragwort, or when rock and hill,
The woods, and distant Skiddaw's lofty height,
Were bronzed with deepest radiance, stood alone
Beneath the sky, as if I had been born
On Indian plains, and from my mother's hut
Had run abroad in wantonness, to sport
A naked savage, in the thunder shower.

(1850 1.288–300)

But that little boy grew up into an adult, and among other kinds of growth he gradually entered the world of adulthood by repeated inoculations of anxiety and guilt in which he eventually lost his sense of innocence. He trapped birds, and then he sometimes took the birds he trapped—"and when the deed was done / I heard among the solitary hills / Loud breathings coming after me" (1.322–24). He plundered birds' nests high on the cliffs and again found himself in frightening solitude: "on the perilous ridge I hung alone" (1.336). He stole a boat and thereby encountered "a darkness, call it a solitude / Or blank desertion" (1.394–95). All these experiences result in solitude, loneliness. And here it matters to recall that the poem "Lucy Gray" is subtitled "Or Solitude" and that Lucy herself is twice called "solitary"; one of the suggestions Wordsworth seems to be making concerns the loneliness and desertion of that which is lost and can never be found again, lost childhood.

The most poignantly personal of all Wordsworth's statements about his own lost childhood is probably in the poem entitled "There Was a Boy." The lines constituting that poem were written in the style of *The Prelude* and are still included there in Book 5. But the poet also published them as a separate piece in the second edition, the "Lucy Gray" edition, of *Lyrical Ballads,* in 1800. In both the 1800 published version and that which eventually appeared in *The Prelude* when it was published in 1850, the boy of Winander seems a definite enough portrait of one of the poet's schoolmates at Hawkshead, so that some critics have actually speculated as to his real identity (see de Selincourt ed. of *Prelude*, 547). But Ms. JJ of *Prelude* pieces, probably written in the fall of 1798 in Germany, roughly the same time and place in which "Lucy Gray" was written, identifies the boy of Winander as Wordsworth himself. We hear him shouting his "mimic hootings" to the owls—"And they would shout / Across the wat'ry vale, and shout again, / Responsive to my call." But there are again moments for this boy when he is deserted, when the owls refuse to hoot back at him and the hills refuse to echo:

> And when it chanced
> That pauses of deep silence mocked my skill,
> Then often in that silence, while I hung
> Listening, a sudden shock of mild surprize
> Would carry far into my heart the voice
> Of mountain torrents.
>> (Ms. JJ.d. 10–12, 15–20, Norton ed., 492)

The "shock of mild surprize" is the shock of a child's discovery that he and the rest of Nature may be, on occasion at least *are*, separate, that the great earthly "heaven" which "lies about us in our infancy," as the poet says in the Ode (67), is not an extension of ourselves, is not fully reliable, may be indeed sometimes hostile. It was, after all, a storm that "came on before

its time'' (29) which killed Lucy Gray, that is, if she *was* killed—
but then only a child would suppose that storms have their
proper "time" and that external Nature is obliged to keep
human rules and expectations and schedules.

"The Boy of Winander" is now included among the Poems
of the Imagination, but in Wordsworth's original proposal of his
plan to Coleridge, in the letter of 1809, he placed it after
"Lucy Gray" and right next to the Intimations Ode in his plan
for the "Poems relating to childhood, and such feelings as arise
in the mind in after life in direct contemplation of that state"
(*MY* 1: 334). When he published the poem in the 1800 *Lyrical
Ballads* volume, and again when he gave it its place in *Prelude* 5,
he made in it what at first glance appears a drastic change, but
in fact a change which brings it into even closer relationship with
"Lucy Gray." He seemingly transformed the boy of Winander
from himself to one of his friends. And then he killed him, and
buried him in the Hawkshead churchyard:

> This boy was taken from his mates, and died
> In childhood, ere he was full twelve years old.
> Pre-eminent in beauty is the vale
> Where he was born and bred: the church-yard
>   hangs
> Upon a slope above the village-school.
> ("There Was a Boy," *PW* 2: 206, lines 26–30)

But this boy of the published poem is *not* really a different person from Wordsworth, any more than Lucy Gray is. He is
Wordsworth's childhood, dead and gone, but not forgotten; contemplated and renewed in contemplation in a way that might

otherwise seem quite morbid in a child mooning in a graveyard. For, says the poet,

> through that churchyard when my way has led
> On summer evenings, I believe, that there
> A long half hour together I have stood
> Mute—looking at the grave in which he lies!
>
> (31–34)

So it is too in the reluctance to decide that Lucy Gray is finally dead, completely and forever lost. It is the Margaret in ourselves that we all mourn for. It is the young William, who continues to exist only in the mind of the man he has become, that Wordsworth mourns for, and evokes.

In their appearance in *The Prelude*, these lines on the boy of Winander are placed so as to make a very particular point. They follow immediately Wordsworth's satiric portrait of a prissy little schoolboy whose education and educators have robbed him of his childhood. "This model of a child," as the poet sarcastically calls him, has been "Full early trained to worship seemliness" (1850 5.29–99). Though without innocence of his own, he "can read lectures upon innocence," for he is "A miracle of scientific lore" (314–15); he is, alas, a product of "unnatural growth," a personification of "Poor human vanity" (328–29). He is, in short, though still young in years and very popular with his throng of adult admirers, more *dead* than the boy of Winander or Lucy Gray, who at least leave behind a lively memory of childhood's spontaneous bliss and vitality. There are worse things for a child to do than not to grow up. As Keats says, there are moments when it indeed seems "rich to die, / To cease upon the midnight with no pain"

("Ode to a Nightingale" 55-56). Far worse, and far more common, is a childhood perverted or brutalized by a materialistic and violent adult society. It could have been a blessing for Lucy Gray that she "never reached the town" (32). As Geoffrey Hartman has wisely remarked on these treatments of childhood, "Wordsworth's . . . theme was growth and immortality, not death" (20).

The effort here is to place the poem "Lucy Gray" in a larger context of Wordsworth's long-continuing poetic efforts to understand and appreciate the motions of the mind which lead from infancy to maturity, and to give permanence to the fleeting joys and powers and innocence of childhood. There is no truer champion in all poetry of that state than Wordsworth, no one who even comes near the kind of epic celebrations of childhood in and of itself which Wordsworth constantly feels and repeatedly expresses. Consider this lofty and utterly convincing passage from *Prelude* 5:

> Our childhood sits,
> Our simple childhood, sits upon a throne
> That hath more power than all the elements.
> I guess not what this tells of Being past,
> Nor what it augurs of the life to come;
> But so it is, and, in that dubious hour,
> That twilight when we first begin to see
> This dawning earth, to recognize, expect,
> And in the long probation that ensues,
> The time of trial, ere we learn to live
> In reconcilement with our stinted powers,
> To endure this state of meagre vassalage;
> Unwilling to forego, confess, submit,

Uneasy and unsettled, yoke-fellows
To custom, mettlesome, and not yet tamed
And humbled down; oh! then we feel, we feel,
We know where we have friends.

(1850 5.507–23)

And yet amid all this general and sublime celebration of childhood, it is essential not to allow "Lucy Gray" to become diluted in an abstract mixture of praise for childhood's joys and melancholic longing for the past and gone. "Lucy Gray" is a genuinely extraordinary individual product of Wordsworth's very individual genius, and not just one more poem on childhood. It has a chilling horror of its own, unique. It has an ironic playfulness which clothes the deepest tragic feelings within our souls. No wonder that when Coleridge came, in his own most profound contemplations, to express the chasm that had by then become obvious between his own condition and poetic attitudes and those of Wordsworth, he focused on "Lucy Gray." Coleridge's state, as he describes it in "Dejection: An Ode," was certainly disastrous for him personally: "afflictions bow me down to earth" (82), and especially the very personal affliction of a suspension of his poetic gift, the suspension of "what nature gave me at my birth, / My shaping spirit of Imagination" (85–86). In this hopeless mood, Coleridge, having learned that not all motions of the mind lead to improvement, seeks the wafting breezes of inspiration and imagination: "Hence, viper thoughts, that coil around my mind, / Reality's dark dream! / I turn from you and listen to the wind" (94–96). And what is to be heard in the wind? At first only ravings and screams of agony, madness and devilish frenzy, pain and shuddering. But Coleridge's ear is well tuned to the wind. And soon he hears, like Elijah in his cave after windstorm and earthquake and fire, a smaller and truer voice:

> But hush! there is a pause of deepest silence!
> And all that noise, as of a rushing crowd,
> With groans, and tremulous shudderings—all is
>   over—
> It tells another tale, with sounds less deep and
>   loud!
> A tale of less affright,
> And tempered with delight,
> As [William's] self had framed the tender lay,—
> 'Tis of a little child
> Upon a lonesome wild,
> Not far from home, but she hath lost her way:
> And now moans low in bitter grief and fear,
> And now screams loud, and hopes to make her
>   mother hear.
> ("Dejection" 114–25; the published version has
> "Otway's" for "William's")

It is not easy to hear the authentic voice within this divine wind. In his brilliant essay "The Correspondent Breeze," Meyer H. Abrams has, better than anyone else, explicated what the voice of the wind means to the Romantic poets, in calling it, among other things, "a ready counterpart for the furor of the inspired poet" (52). But the difficulty with the voice of the wind is that it comes as a *mixture* of sounds and images and messages. Coleridge knew this, too, as he puts this great complication into the simple words of his Ancient Mariner, who describes *his* encounter with the wind:

It raised my hair, it fanned my cheek
Like a meadow-gale of spring—
It mingled strangely with my fears
Yet it felt like a welcoming.

(456–59)

And this, finally, is the greatest of Wordsworth's accomplishments in "Lucy Gray," the poetic and educational achievement "embodied in the mystery of words." Wordsworth accepts the ambiguity of the dead child who can never more be seen but who *is* seen. He accepts the uncertainty; indeed, he insists on it, he champions it. It is the achievement of permanence, after all, for the fleeting. It is the vision of eternity encased in mutability. It is the successful enlarging of the circle of sensibilities for the mind in motion. And it is unique, "a solitary song":

O'er rough and smooth she trips along,
And never looks behind;
And sings a solitary song
That whistles in the wind.

(61–64)

CHAPTER SIX

Inducing "Exquisite Regard for Common Things"

Not everybody likes Wordsworth's poetry yet; but in those closing years of the eighteenth century, when he was first bursting on the literary scene, there were probably at least as many people who wished he had never burst as there were sympathetic readers to welcome him and his poetry into print. Typical of many was the greeting expressed on the subject of the *Lyrical Ballads* in the *Monthly Review* of June 1799 by Dr. Charles Burney, the father of the famous novelist Fanny Burney and in his day a famous music teacher and man of taste, who Dr. Johnson once said was "a man for all the world to love." Dr. Burney was generous enough to end his 1799 review by saying, "So much genius and originality are discovered in this publication, that we wish to see another from the same hand" (210). But the details of his remarks on the *Lyrical Ballads* make it clear that he awaited more of Wordsworth's poems not because he was delighted by those he had seen but because he was displeased and disappointed. He gives a generally obtuse reading of most of the poems in the volume, dismissing, for example, Coleridge's *Rime of the Ancient Mariner* as "the strangest story of a cock and bull that we ever saw on paper, . . . a rhapsody of unintelligible wildness and incoherence" (204).

But it is in what Burney says of Wordsworth's "Tintern Abbey" that we may see something more than obtuseness. What we may see is a mind so solidified, not in ignorance by any means, but in knowledgeable complacency, that it would take a genuine revolution to open new awareness in such a mentality.

"Tintern Abbey," says Burney, trying to be fair, is "poetical, beautiful, and philosophical." But the poetry, the beauty, the philosophy—especially the philosophy—all fail because the poet has missed the central truth about Nature, and about human nature, according to the critic. Burney rejects Wordsworth's "gloomy, narrow, and unsocial ideas of seclusion from the commerce of the world: as if men were born to live in woods and wilds unconnected with each other!" (210). The reviewer, the good doctor, here speaks for more than himself; he becomes the conscience and voice of the waning eighteenth century and of the great Literary Club and the Age of Johnson.

All good men knew then, and had known for a long time, that poetry and philosophy go hand in hand and that both are chiefly *academic*. Education is the highest proof of civilization, and poetry is the highest flowering of the educated mind. And education is truly and only *academic*, of the academy. Education is schooling. A poet who writes beautifully has learned to do so in school. A poet who observes beauty in Nature and who gains inspiration from that beauty has learned to do those things in school too. In Dr. Burney's own words on "Tintern Abbey,"

> Is it not to education and the culture of the mind that we owe the raptures which the author so well describes, as arising from the view of beautiful scenery, and sublime objects of nature enjoyed in tranquility, when contrasted with the artificial machinery and 'busy hum of men' in a city? The savage sees none of the beauties which this author describes. (210)

Wordsworth's attempt, which to Burney seems misadvised, in "Tintern Abbey" to reduce civilization in the Wye River Valley to no more than the presence of temporarily trespassing gypsies, "vagrant dwellers in the houseless woods" (line 20), and a lone hermit dwelling in a cave is all bad enough. But his claim that it is Nature, not even human nature and certainly not the schools, that provides the link between his human soul and the beauteous forms that he perceives in Nature,

> the meadows and the woods,
> And mountains; and . . . all that we behold
> from this green earth
>
> (103–05)

—that is simply too much. Burney knew, and so did his world, that education is a human achievement, and it is man-made. It is exactly what Wordsworth allows Matthew to call it in his poem "Expostulation and Reply," that is, "that light bequeathed" from men to men through social institutions, through schools and libraries, "To Beings else forlorn and blind" (5–6).

Dr. Burney's intentions were generous, and he tried to be appreciative. But Wordsworth's claims were impossibly beyond him. "Tintern Abbey," he reluctantly concluded, is a mistake, but it represents "the reflections of no common mind" (210).

It is that final assumption of uniqueness and eliteness, of uncommonness, that Wordsworth might well have found most objectionable in Dr. Burney's review. For Wordsworth was militantly and enduringly *common*. One of his most striking and most frequent claims is to be the purveyor of the reflections of a *common* mind, especially reflections on how common minds, like his, gain their education *out* of school, from common things.

"Higher minds," Wordsworth observes near the end of his poetic study of his own mind and its education, possess the ability to

> build up greatest things
> From least suggestions; ever on the watch,
> Willing to work and to be wrought upon,
> They need not extraordinary calls
> To rouse them.
>
> (1850 *Prelude* 14.101–05)

Wordsworth himself, although he championed the common mind, of course also possessed one of these "higher minds." And Wordsworth himself is also well described by his famous definition of a poet: "He is a man speaking to men: a man, it is true, endowed with more lively sensibility, more enthusiasm and tenderness, who has a greater knowledge of human nature, and a more comprehensive soul, than are supposed to be common among mankind" (*Prose* 1: 138). So then a poet, a Wordsworth, in his own words is a higher mind, with at least a seemingly uncommon sensibility and enthusiasm and knowledge.

And yet even in this context of intellectual superiority, there is in Wordsworth an insistent *commonness* which is constantly startling. That insistent rejection of any need for "extraordinary calls" near the end of *The Prelude* is typical of this commonness, and the wording of the Preface to *Lyrical Ballads* about what is "supposed to be common among mankind" suggests a distrust of any negative suppositions about the common.

The insistent ordinariness of Wordsworth, although it has been shown to have familiar roots in a literary tradition which had developed in England by the end of the eighteenth century (see Jordan, "The Novelty," and Ryskamp), has no parallel among the major English poets who preceded him. Much can be seen in the way poets employ, or avoid, the common. Wordsworth very knowingly threw down a gauntlet of revolutionary poetics and education when he announced that the "principal object" of the *Lyrical Ballads* was "to choose incidents and situations" and language "from common life" (*Prose* 1: 123). He proclaimed himself a champion of the common, and he was the first great poet to offer such a proclamation. It was one of his early convictions. In later years, when his attachment to the common perhaps began to lose some of its strength in the period of early manhood, as he tells us near the end of *The Prelude*, his sister Dorothy reentered his life and helped to reinforce, as he says, what was always for him a necessary "sense / Of exquisite regard for common things" (14.261–62).

There is no such expression "of exquisite regard for common things" in Shakespeare, for example. He expresses a much more traditional view when, in Sonnet 102, he writes that "sweets grown common lose their dear delight" (12). And characters in Shakespeare's plays disdain the common. One thinks, for example, of the Prince of Arragon in *The Merchant of Venice*, who proclaims before Portia's caskets:

> I will not choose what many men desire,
> Because I will not jump with common spirits,
> And rank me with the barbarous multitudes.
> (2.9.31–33)

Still less of an admirer of the common is Shakespeare's Coriolanus, who banishes from his presence all his inferiors as he barks,

"You common cry of curs, whose breath I hate / As reek o' th' rotten fens" (3.3.120-21). And Prince Hamlet uses the very word *common* as one of his verbal daggers when first his mother and then her new husband try to persuade him that "death of fathers" is the "common theme" of Heaven, Nature, Reason (1.2.103-04), a perfectly ordinary fact which "is as common / As any the most vulgar thing to sense" (1.2.98-99); and Hamlet disagreeably agrees: "Ay, madam, it is common" (1.2.74).

Milton, so often Wordsworth's model in important ways, does not even use the word *common* in his poetry in the sense of "ordinary." No one would ever call Milton a poet of the ordinary. He speaks of such things as our "common Prison" (*Samson*, line 6, also 1161) or our "common enemy" (*Samson* 1416), but he certainly does not ever reveal any "exquisite regard for common things."

Alexander Pope, though he aims at poetic expression of universal truths, avoids the ordinary and advises his readers to do likewise. Genius does not loiter in common paths, as he explains in his *Essay on Criticism*:

> Thus Pegasus, a nearer way to take,
> May boldly deviate from the common track;
> From vulgar bounds with brave disorder
>   part,
> And snatch a grace beyond the reach of art,
> Which, without passing through the judgment,
>   gains
> The heart, and all its end at once attains.
> In prospects, thus, some objects please our eyes,
> Which out of nature's common order rise.
>   (150-57)

This is quite different from Wordsworth, for whom the most pleasing prospects are those which are full of, not out of, "nature's common order."

It is worth noting here that Wordsworth's theorizing about the common and his poetic depicting of the ordinary did not entirely overthrow this traditional disdain for the common among great poets. The Revolution of Ordinariness was by no means total in its triumph. Wordsworth has certainly had his important followers, Walt Whitman for one very notable example. But for many poets, poetry remains an elitist realm. Robert Southey, for an early example among the opponents of the ordinary, complained early and loud that Wordsworth was writing about "uninteresting subjects" (204). And as Lord Byron looked back over the course of his own poetic voyages, he boasted, "At least I have shunn'd the common shore" (*DJ* 10.27). Such pride as Byron's in being uncommon is not far removed, either in the timing of its public appearance in *Don Juan* or in basic meaning and attitude, from Coleridge's attack in the 1817 *Biographia Literaria* on what he calls Wordsworth's "matter-of-factness" and "*mental* bombast," exemplified for Coleridge in Wordsworth's allowing something so rarefied and sublime as the "bliss of solitude" to arise out of memories of something so commonplace as daffodils (*BL*, ed. Shawcross 2: 101–03, 109–10).

But Wordsworth was not easily deterred by precedent, or friend, or foe. In 1819, two years after Coleridge published his discussion of Wordsworth's "characteristic defects," Wordsworth let fly with the poem *Peter Bell*, which he had long withheld from public view. There in his preface he admitted that, like the earlier Coleridge, who also knew how to sympathize with jackasses, "I was put upon writing the poem out of liking

for the creature [the common donkey] that is so often so
dreadfully abused." And nearby, in the Prologue to *Peter Bell*,
Wordsworth announced his defiance of expectations of poetic
elitism. The crescent moon of flying imagination that he
characterizes in that Prologue offers the poet extraordinary
calls—"the secrets of a land / Where human foot did never stray"
(96–97), or "the realm of Faery, / Among the lovely shades of
things" (101–02), or "Less quiet regions . . . of magic lore"
(107–10). But the poet rejects all that exotic stuff, all that material
which could serve a Keats or a Shelley or Coleridge himself so
well. Says Wordsworth:

> Long have I loved, what I behold,
> The night that calms, the day that cheers;
> The common growth of mother-earth
> Suffices me—her tears, her mirth,
> Her humblest mirth and tears.
>
> The dragon's wing, the magic ring,
> I shall not covet for my dower,
> If I along that lowly way
> With sympathetic heart may stray,
> And with a soul of power.
>
> These given, what more need I desire
> To stir, to soothe, or elevate?
> What nobler marvels than the mind
> May in life's daily prospect find,
> May find or there create?
>
> (131–45)

So conditioned are we still, and so conditioned was the reading public in Wordsworth's day, to expecting not inspiration but dullness in commonplace things and situations that Wordsworth found in his efforts to make poetry out of the commonplace a sense of crusade that would stay with him for a lifetime. It was not a mere matter of preference with him, however. He showed a determination not to neglect or lose any source of knowledge or insight. And as a self-proclaimed Prophet of Nature, he found it essential in his role of man speaking to men to omit nothing from his poetry that could benefit and enlighten his readers. "To me the meanest flower that blows can give / Thoughts that do often lie too deep for tears," he writes at the end of the Intimations Ode. That fact being established, it follows that Wordsworth in his poetry must examine with close scrutiny the meanest flower—indeed, all flowers and all other common things. He must not miss the deep thoughts they can give. And as a poet he feels the responsibility to convey those thoughts to his readers without loss or omission. And also without false excitement, without spectacular screams for attention. "I have wished to keep the reader in the company of flesh and blood," he announces in the Preface to *Lyrical Ballads* (*Prose* 1: 131), and that intention, as he reminds us there, means an avoidance of the "frantic" and the "sickly" and the "extravagant." He wants always to "counteract" in his readers the "degrading thirst after outrageous stimulation" (*Prose* 1: 129–31).

It is essential, therefore, to explore this Wordsworthian cultivation of the commonplace—attempting to find out what the common things of earth meant to this uncommon poet, what lessons he learned from the meanest flowers, and what and how he expected his readers to gain from his poetic treatments of "the common growth of mother-earth."

The earliest lesson that Wordsworth learned from common things was in some ways the greatest. By observing the things of earth the *child* Wordsworth saw too or seemed to see the very face of heaven. The great Ode begins with this memory:

> There was a time when meadow, grove, and
> stream,
> The earth, and every common sight
> To me did seem
> Apparelled in celestial light.
>
> (1–4)

Nor is this vision splendid a private one. The poet insists that this ability of "every common sight" on earth to convey to children the vision of heaven is universal. "Heaven lies about us in our infancy!" (67)—it lies about us *all*.

But of course it does not stay with us, not with our conscious perceptions, and the *loss* of heaven in later years is also universal. There comes a time to every one of us when, thinking of the scenes of heaven, we must admit:

> It is not now as it hath been of yore:—
> Turn whereso'er I may,
> By night or day,
> The things which I have seen I now can see no
> more.
>
> (6–9)

Now it is true, the poet tells us, that we retain some indistinct memories of that celestial period of earth life:

> O joy! that in our embers
> Is something that doth live,

That Nature yet remembers
What was so fugitive!
(130–33)

There is for him and, he says, for us all a sense of "perpetual
benediction" (135) in those memories, despite their blurred
vagueness:

Those shadowy recollections,
Which, be they what they may,
Are yet the fountain light of all our day,
Are yet a master light of all our seeing.
(150–53)

But this claim begins, for all its poetic beauty—maybe because
of all its poetic beauty—to sound like *too much* poetry, like the
airy and insubstantial product of a poet's eye, in a fine frenzy
rolling, glancing from heaven to earth, from earth to heaven,
and having no real contact with the common life of this planet,
no solid connection with "the common growth of mother-earth"
to which Wordsworth claims to maintain allegiance.

But no. On the contrary, Wordsworth rarely loses that contact with common reality, and never for very long. The celestial
glory of the earth in our childhood is a common reality for him.
And just exactly what happens to the celestial light that once
has been the very apparel of "every common sight"? How does
the vague recollection of a light that is gone function still as "the
fountain light of all our day" and "a master light of all our seeing"? The answer is pure Wordsworth, and crucial. The light
of the heavenly vision does not die, although to the perception
of men it *seems* to "die away." It does not fade away, either.

In modern cinema or television parlance, the technique of "fade-in" produces the gradual coming or bringing into full visibility of an image. Wordsworth uses the same language to describe the same kind of process. The visionary celestial light of heaven on earth, he says, which seems to die away, actually fades "into the light of common day." The celestial light *merges* into and becomes absorbed by that very Wordsworthian-sounding "master light of all our seeing," "the light of common day." This light, common daylight, is one of the poet's favorite images and the very similar phrases he uses to describe it again and again are among his favorite words.

Wordsworth's own life and poetic career must be viewed in this heavenly "light of common day." And once that light is shone upon him, how revelatory it is of his highest experiences and perceptions, of his education. His description of himself in *The Prelude* as a ten-year-old boy, with his insistent founding of his childhood joys in the commonplace, is a good example:

> Thus oft amid those fits of vulgar joy
> Which, through all seasons, on a child's pursuits
> Are prompt attendants, 'mid that giddy bliss
> Which, like a tempest, works along the blood
> And is forgotten; even then I felt
> Gleams like the flashing of a shield;—the earth
> And common face of Nature spake to me
> Rememberable things.
>
> (1.581–88)

Another example comes out of Wordsworth's poetic description of his years at Hawkshead. He describes his youthful excursion to Furness Abbey (a place that could conjure up most extraordinary feelings and experiences), and another excursion to Bowness and the old White Lion Inn, and a boat race on Windermere out to Lady Holm Isle, and so on—all of these experiences that might inspire poetic gushing. But for Wordsworth it is invariably the ordinary aspects of these potentially exotic places and experiences, *not* the extraordinary, that are of most meaning. He summarizes their effects on him in these words:

> Thus were my sympathies enlarged, and thus
> Daily the common range of visible things
> Grew dear to me; already I began
> To love the sun; a boy I loved the sun
> Not as I since have loved him, as a pledge
> And surety of our earthly life, a light
> Which we behold and feel we are alive;
> Nor for his bounty to so many worlds—
> But for this cause, that I had seen him lay
> His beauty on the morning hills, had seen
> The western mountains touch his setting orb,
> In many a thoughtless hour, when from excess
> Of happiness, my blood appeared to flow
> For its own pleasure, and I breathed with joy.
>
> (2.175–88)

His joys derive from the circulation of common blood through common veins, the breathing of common air in common lungs. It is again and again "the light of common day" that illuminates the poet's vision.

There is more to all this constant examination of common things by common light than simple admiration, however sublime. For Wordsworth's education was dependent on his association with the common face of earth. There is no reason to detract, though he himself sometimes does, from the unusually good schooling he obtained at Hawkshead and even, despite its problems in the late eighteenth century, at Cambridge. But there is no doubt that he himself believed that, whatever the quality and advantages of his formal schooling, his greatest education lay elsewhere. Academic "glory," he tells us, "was but little sought by me, / And little won" (*Prelude* 3.74–75). At Cambridge particularly he repeatedly had "A feeling that I was not for that hour, / Nor for that place" (3.81–82), a feeling that drove him out alone into the fields outside of Cambridge, where

> As if awakened, summoned, roused, constrained,
> I looked for universal things; perused
> The common countenance of earth and sky
> (3.108–10)

and found in that common countenance of earth and sky a lingering celestial light—and an education not offered at Cambridge or any other university. He sought from common things to learn—and from them he *did* learn—highest truth: "I called on both [heaven and earth] to teach me what they might; / Or turning the mind in upon herself," for the internal landscape for Wordsworth was inseparable from the rest of the common countenance of earth and sky,

> Pored, watched, expected, listened, spread my
>   thoughts
> And spread them with a wider creeping; felt
> Incumbencies more awful, visitings

Of the Upholder, of the tranquil soul,
That tolerates the indignities of Time,
And, from the centre of Eternity
All finite motions overruling, lives
In glory immutable. But peace! enough
Here to record I had ascended now
To such community with highest truth.
(3.115–26)

Not all of his education from earth's commonplace was so determinedly active or required such pursuit and striving. One of the crucial educational experiences of the poet's life came to him when he was *not* engaged in any conscious effort

to exalt the mind
By solitary study, to uphold
Intense desire through meditative peace.
(4.304–06)

It is an account that achieves that perfectly Wordsworthian blend of the personal, the unique, the singled out, but also the very common:

The cock had crowed, and now the eastern sky
Was kindling, not unseen, from humble copse
And open field, through which the pathway
    wound,
And homeward led my steps. Magnificent
The morning rose, in memorable pomp,
Glorious as e'er I had beheld—in front,
The sea lay laughing at a distance; near

The solid mountains shone, bright as the clouds,
Grain-tinctured, drenched in empyrean light;
And in the meadows and the lower grounds
Was all the sweetness of a common dawn—
Dews, vapours, and the melody of birds,
And labourers going forth to till the fields.
Ah! need I say, dear Friend! that to the brim
My heart was full; I made no vows, but vows
Were then made for me; bond unknown to me
Was given, that I should be, else sinning greatly,
A dedicated Spirit.

(4.320–37)

This is surely an extraordinary moment in the life of anyone, including any poet. But even this extraordinary instant of vow-making and dedication, of poetic ordination, does not result from any extraordinary call. The morning was magnificent and glorious, but not the *most* glorious of all time—just "glorious as e'er I had beheld." The dawn *within* the poet was surely uncommon, but it took place in "all the sweetness of a common dawn." No senate crowned the poet; no synod anointed him. His companions were "Dews, vapours, and the melody of birds, / And labourers going forth to till the fields"—common labourers, of course, and common birds, appropriate to that common dawn.

To whatever degree contact with common things educates—seeing things in a common light of day, awakening with a common dawn—to a similar degree being cut off from those common contacts can prevent learning, can even, in extreme cases, destroy the mind. Thus Vaudracour, in one sense an extreme extension of Wordsworth himself, but also a representative of the "last recess" of human woe—thwarted, utterly frustrated, damned—reaches at last a condition of "shunning even the light of common day" (1805 *Prelude* 9.909, 930). Thus cut off from that common "light of all our seeing," he can be touched or affected or educated by nothing at all, not even "the voice of freedom," nor "public hope, / Or personal memory of his own deep wrongs." Without that common association, having lost "the light of common day," Vaudracour, and anyone like him, reverts to mental nonbeing: "In those gloomy shades, / His days he wasted, an imbecile mind" (9.581-85).

Vaudracour does represent an extreme case of human suffering. He is not Everyman. He is not Wordsworth, at least mostly not. There would be no point in mentioning him here, with all his shunning of "the light of common day," when the aim is to trace for a moment what the poet owed to his contacts with common things, except that Wordsworth had his own kinds of Vaudracour-like periods, when he too sank in disillusionment and depression into

> The couch his fate had made for him; supine,
> Save when the stings of viperous remorse
> Trying their strength, enforced him to start up,
> Aghast and [possibly, in Wordsworth's case, at
>   times] prayerless.
>
> (9.575-78)

It was out of some such moral crisis that Dorothy brought her brother back to himself. And, inevitably, her tools were the common things of earth. At a time when the poet's soul had become too severe, too over-stern, too solid and terrible a rock, he tells her,

Thou didst plant its crevices with flowers,
Hang it with shrubs that twinkle in the breeze,
And teach the little birds to build their nests
And warble in its chambers. At a time
When Nature, destined to remain so long
Foremost in my affections, had fallen back
Into a second place, pleased to become
When every day brought with it some new sense
Of exquisite regard for common things
And all the earth was budding with these gifts
A handmaid to a nobler than herself,
Of more refined humanity, thy breath,
Dear Sister! was a kind of gentler spring
That went before my steps.

(14.253–66)

Thus recalled to himself and the truest bases of his knowledge and education and human concern, Wordsworth could learn his greatest lessons of truth. And the truth that continually mattered most to him was common truth, as he says in the 1850 Preface to *Lyrical Ballads*—truth "not individual and local, but general and operative" (*Prose* 1: 139). And knowledge of such truth both creates and is a product of joy, or of pleasure. The two terms *joy* and *pleasure* are not exactly synonymous, but there are places where Wordsworth seems to use them to mean virtually the same thing. Knowledge amounts to awareness of common principles, and it springs from joy. In the same Preface, he writes, "We have no knowledge, that is, no general principles drawn from the contemplation of particular facts, but what has been built up by pleasure, and exists in us by pleasure alone" (*Prose* 1: 140). The language in *The Prelude*, Book 8, is really quite similar. In the 1805 *Prelude*, Wordsworth speaks of "two principles of joy" (8.173), and in both the 1805 and 1850 versions he identifies those "two principles of joy," out of which knowledge comes, as "the common haunts of the green earth" and the "ordinary interests of men" (1850, 8.116–17). "Common haunts," ordinary human concerns, these things are the only reliable paths to joy, and joy is the prerequisite to knowledge, to learning. Educational theory has here come a very long way from the received opinions expressed by Dr. Charles Burney in his 1799 review of Wordsworth's poems.

As *The Prelude* tells the story, the culminating educational experience of Wordsworth's mental development occurred at Mt. Snowdon. Here in his descriptions of this experience, the crucial tension inherent in Wordsworth's theories about the sublime and the commonplace as somehow one becomes most apparent. The Snowdon vision is itself a representation of "the enduring and the transient" (14.100). It is impressive, spectacular, and immensely individual. It is a once-in-a-lifetime event, or rather rarer yet, for Wordsworth compares it to the once-in-all-time creation of the world. The very rhythms and sounds of the poetry aim at conveying the sharp and sudden impact and uniqueness of this grandest of moments, this extraordinary and highly uncommon event in human history:

> I remember well
> That in life's every-day appearances
> I seemed about this time to gain clear sight
> Of a new world—a world, too, that was fit
> To be transmitted, and to other eyes
> Made visible; as ruled by those fixed laws
> Whence spiritual dignity originates,

Which do both give it being and maintain
A balance, an ennobling interchange
Of actions from without and from within;
The excellence, pure function, and best power
Both of the object seen, and eye that sees.

(13.367–78)

For Wordsworth, the spectacle he witnessed atop Mt. Snowdon would inevitably come "in life's every-day appearances." It is the commonplace object that calls forth both the excellence and best power of the seeing eye.

And such extraordinary visions, as they continued to come to the poet in later years, retained that firm foundation in the commonplace. One such, for example, was of a Scottish girl, a Highland girl, encountered near Loch Lomond during the tour that William and Dorothy and Coleridge took in the late summer of 1803. That vision, the poet told Isabella Fenwick four decades later, remained for him "a most vivid remembrance," an extraordinary occurrence but with the expectably Wordsworthian ordinary bases:

Sweet Highland Girl, a very shower
Of beauty is thy earthly dower!
Twice seven consenting years have shed
Their utmost bounty on thy head:
And these grey rocks; that household lawn;
Those trees, a veil just half withdrawn;
This fall of water that doth make
A murmur near the silent lake;
This little bay; a quiet road
That holds in shelter thy Abode—

In truth together do ye seem
Like something fashioned in a dream;
Such forms as from their covert peep
When earthly cares are laid asleep!
But, O fair Creature! in the light
Of common day, so heavenly bright,
I bless Thee, Vision as thou art,
I bless thee with a human heart.
("To a Highland Girl," PW 3: 73-75, lines 1-18)

How typically and appropriately Wordsworthian is the tension within the phrase "the light / Of common day, so heavenly bright"!

But important as it is to discover how Wordsworth himself arrived at the truths he learned, there is something still more important to observe here—something crucial for understanding *how* to read Wordsworth and *what* to read him for. That "clear sight / Of a new world" which arose for him on Snowdon out of "life's everyday appearances" had the very important quality of being sharable. It was

a world, too, that was fit
To be transmitted, and to other eyes
Made visible.
(1850 13.368-72)

That is, it was a vision given not only for the poet's personal education and edification but for his poetry, for that greater purpose of enabling him to be, *on the subject of this vision*, a man speaking to men. And this capability of transmitting truths in Wordsworth's poetry remains tied to the necessary, exquisite regard for common things, for life's everyday appearances. On this element, so essential to both his style and his subject matter, the poet insists. Witness in this very context and in adjacent lines Wordsworth's statement on how his early poetry caught and taught one of the most important of his early audience, Coleridge. When Coleridge first heard the poem *Adventures on Salisbury Plain*, both he and Wordsworth tell us, he was much struck by the newness of Wordsworth's method of deriving lofty and universal truth from the familiar, the commonplace. *The Prelude* describes the method and Coleridge's response like this:

> And thou, O Friend!
> Pleased with some unpremeditated strains
> That served those wanderings to beguile, hast said
> That then and there my mind had exercised
> Upon the vulgar forms of present things,
> The actual world of our familiar days,
> Yet higher power; had caught from them a tone,
> An image, and a character, by books
> Not hitherto reflected.
>
> (13.352–60)

Coleridge's own words, in Chapter 4 of *Biographia Literaria*, make the same point about his response; he was not merely enthusiastic but was especially struck by the appearance of great truths from amid things of custom, "the actual world of our familiar days":

> It was not . . . the freedom from false taste . . .
> which made so unusual an impression on my

feelings immediately, and subsequently on my judgment. It was the union of deep feeling with profound thought; the fine balance of truth in observing with the imaginative faculty in modifying the objects observed; and above all the original gift of spreading the tone, the *atmosphere* and with it the depth and height of the ideal world, around forms, incidents, and situations of which, for the common view, custom had bedimmed all the lustre, had dried up the sparkle and the dewdrops. (*BL*, ed. Shawcross 1: 59)

Most striking to Coleridge in the poetry of this early Wordsworth, he says, was Wordsworth's genius "to carry on the feelings of childhood into the powers of manhood; to combine the child's sense of wonder and novelty with the appearances which every day for perhaps forty years had rendered familiar" (1: 59). Coleridge knew at once that one of the chief virtues of Wordsworth's poetic teachings, and certainly one of their most original, was their foundation in the familiar but somehow heretofore unseen or inadequately observed.

At least in those early years, Coleridge's response helped to set Wordsworth on his continuing course by giving him assurance that there really was a fit audience for him, that there really were readers who could discover by what species of courtesy his attempts at poetry could be called poetic and how those attempts could be seen as fitting into and continuing the traditions of English poetry while at the same time making so utterly new a departure into the glorification of the commonplace, a realm largely unexplored by the great English poets who preceded him.

For, gratifying as Coleridge's early response must have been, Wordsworth wanted more; he wanted a reading *public*. He wanted *us*. He felt the need to teach us all, in Blake's phrase, "To see a World in a grain of Sand" ("Auguries of Innocence," 1). With Wordsworth we are challenged repeatedly, constantly, almost endlessly, to learn in the same way that Coleridge learned—to find among the common things of common life, and each for our own peculiar private self, the ordinary which is both universal and true.

Many of the poet's most valuable teaching moments come in what in *The Prelude* he calls "spots of time," of which many are recorded in that poem but of which numerous equivalents, not so labelled, he offers in other poems too. These "spots of time" are those encounters with life that leave lasting and beneficent effects on our minds because of their clarity and sharp focus and strength. The effects are beneficial; the poet wavered between calling them "fructifying" for the mind, in 1799 (1799 *Prelude* 1.190), and "renovating," in later years (1805 *Prelude* 11.259; 1850, 12.210). As Wordsworth defines and describes "spots of time," it seems fair to say that many poems outside the actual *Prelude* qualify: the encounter with the daffodils, for example, in "I Wandered Lonely as a Cloud," or the meeting with the seemingly "oldest man that ever wore grey hairs" in "Resolution and Independence," or even the chance sighting by break of day the solitary child Lucy Gray, or the revisit to the banks of the Wye near Tintern Abbey in 1798, or the conversation with the grey-headed Shepherd who told of Hart-Leap Well.

Every one of these "spots of time" seems somehow immense and unique. The poet himself says that they are always characterized by "distinct pre-eminence" (12.209) and that they lift us out of the depression "of ordinary intercourse" (12.214). So far they sound not as if they exemplify that insistent Wordsworthian ordinariness, but as if they actually contradict it. But Wordsworth, here above all, remains consistently, as Mary Jacobus has called him, "the poet of the everyday" (7). The lessons we learn from "spots of time" are exalting and extraordinary, but the opportunities for them are utterly commonplace, by no means rare. "Such moments / Are scattered everywhere," *The Prelude* tells us (12.223–24), and indeed Wordsworth is as much the poet of the everywhere and the everything as of the everyday.

What does the poet gain from this perception of the commonplace? Or what does he intend for his readers to gain? It is useful to offer two main suggestions.

First, and typical of Wordsworth as educator, he intends to offer not so much description as provocation. *His* "spots of time," which he shares so abundantly, are meant chiefly as examples and encouragement to us to come up with our own bases of mental repair and nourishment. This kind of sharing and encouraging and provoking is surely one of the ways, as he writes, that

> feeling comes in aid
> Of feeling, and diversity of strength
> Attends us.
>
> (12.269–71)

It is not enough, not at all, to remain with Wordsworth's poetry merely a passive reader, any more than it was sufficient for him to be merely a passive observer of Nature. How often he writes of the needed combination of perceiving *and* creating, or at least half-creating ("Tintern Abbey," 106–07), the combination of sensing both the external breeze, "the sweet breath of heaven," as it blows on our body, and also the "correspondent breeze" *within* and its "quickening virtue" (*Prelude* 1.33–36). Speaking of the "fructifying" or "renovating" experiences which he calls "spots of time," Wordsworth addresses the individual human being with this apt warning; "I . . . see. . . ," he says,

> something of the base
> On which thy greatness stands; but this I feel,
> That from thyself it comes, that thou must give,
> Else never canst receive.
>
> (12.273–77)

We must, then, each seek, find, and experience our own "spots of time." Wordsworth shows us how by citing some of his own examples. But perhaps even more important, he shows us again and again *where* to look for these extraordinary lessons: everywhere, in common things, in all that we behold.

The second notion underlying Wordsworth's commonplaceness is that he insists everywhere on a philosophical attitude which has a common and much-used name but which actually occurs among the vast collections of human convictions in great rarity. This is the attitude of *democracy*.

At the beginning of his literary career, in 1794, Wordsworth wrote to William Matthews:

> Here at the very threshold I solemnly affirm that in no writing of mine will I ever admit of any sentiment which can have the least tendency to induce my readers to suppose that the doctrines

[i.e., of despotism] which are now enforced by banishment, imprisonment, &c, &c, are other than pregnant with every species of misery. You know perhaps already that I am of that odious class of men called democrats, and of that class I shall for ever continue. (*EY* 119)

But that solemn declaration of 1794 troubles some people. It can only "be read with shame and sadness in the light of Wordsworth's subsequent career," presumably meaning a subsequent career of Toryism and poet-laureateship, says one twentieth-century critic (Elwin 44). And in the past century and a half, and more, there have indeed been numerous indictments, some of them sad, of Wordsworth as an apostate, a failed democrat. He has been attacked by spokesmen for major political parties of quite different points of view, and his political statements and actions have very often evoked dismay and even horror from such wise men as Byron and Shelley and Browning and a host of critics. But to call Wordsworth an advocate of democracy is not necessarily to speak about politics. It is to speak about his convictions of mind, his philosophical underpinnings in favor of common things and common people that could no more be eroded by the excesses of the French Revolution or the snarliness of the Alfoxden neighbors than his love for "shepherds, dwellers in the valleys" (*Michael* 23) could ever be undermined by the fact that sheep can be stupid and smelly animals. Wordsworth knew common people as well and as intimately as he knew common things. He also had a good deal of experience, especially for one of his economic station, with *un*common people—the rich, the powerful, the obliging. His preference remained always for the common, for the truly, not merely politically, *democratic* view. He describes in *The Prelude* how as the French Revolution developed and evolved he found that

> every thing was wanting that might give
> Courage to them who looked for good by light
> Of rational Experience, for the shoots
> And hopeful blossoms of a second spring.
>
> (11.3–6)

But if the Revolution and succession of regimes and severed heads offered no hope, "in me," he says, "confidence was unimpaired" (11.7). Wordsworth's democratic faith and philosophy had remarkably little to do with governments and politics. "In the People was my trust," he affirms simply (11.11), but it was an affirmation that few politicians of any brand and none of Wordsworth's political detractors could make so convincingly. And years later, at the time of the Peninsular Wars and the newly hatched tyranny of Napoleon Bonaparte, the poet remained true to his democratic principles. "In despite of the mightiest power which a foreign Invader" or any other source of oppression can bring to bear, he writes in his *Convention of Cintra* tract in 1809, "the cause of the People, in dangers and difficulties issuing from this quarter of oppression, is safe while it remains not only in the bosom but in the hands of the People" (*Prose* 1: 154).

There is little encouragement for politicians of any stripe in Wordsworth's writings. In that same 1794 letter to William Matthews, he spoke with disgust of "the infatuation profligacy and extravagance of men in power" (*EY* 119). And it is perhaps lamentably true that political thinkers will never respond very warmly to Wordsworth's nonpartisan but genuinely social democratic reverence, a reverence for the common things and common people of the earth, that ingredient in his writing which William Hazlitt, who nevertheless became another of Wordsworth's political detractors, rightly hailed as the *philosophical* basis of Wordsworth's poetry, that democratizing insistence which claims "kindred only with the commonest" (5: 163).

Wordsworth's ordinariness, his constant and insistent demand that the greatest beauty and the greatest truths are perceived by "the light of common day" and are expressed in the terminology of common speech, is at once both the most revolutionary and the most fundamental of the insights that underlie his work. Today, great poetry has not much of mass appeal. As in Charles Burney's eighteenth century, poetry today most often appeals to an elitist and academic audience. Readers of poetry who tend to enjoy Wordsworth's poetry the most tend also to be uncommon in education and experience and taste. Readers of his, or any, poetry are too likely to pride themselves on their knowledge and awareness, on their elevation above the common herd. Perhaps it may be Wordsworth's greatest difficulty for readers that he insists on that exquisite regard for common things. But it may also be his greatest value—to preserve us from the fate of Vaudracour, who, arriving at a stage where he was "Cut off from all intelligence with man, / And shunning even the light of common day," became a soul untouchable by natural education, unreachable by truth: "His days he wasted, an imbecile mind!" Reading Wordsworth by "light of common day" can keep us from that condition, can keep our minds in a state of growth. That common light, as it turns out, is the light we too often shun, and the one light we cannot do without.

CHAPTER SEVEN

Ambiguity, Antinarration, Subversion

For setting and keeping the mind in motion, it is hard to imagine a technique more effective than poetic ambiguity. Certainly that is a technique very dear to Wordsworth, as has been observed in preceding discussions of such poems as ''Hart-Leap Well'' and the ''Song at the Feast of Brougham Castle'' and *The Idiot Boy* (see chapters 1, 2, and 4). But no work of Wordsworth's plunges his readers into more unsettling ambiguity, and no work has perhaps had so subversive and revolutionary an effect on readers' expectations and poets' experiments than ''The Thorn,'' one of the poems originally collected for the *Lyrical Ballads* of 1798. It is a poem of immense significance not only for what it can do for the motions of the minds of Wordsworth's readers but also for the astonishing influence it has exercised on other writers, beginning in Wordsworth's own time, in the development of fresh approaches to poetic and narrative techniques. Wordsworth always had in mind his role as teacher and exemplar to ''youthful Poets,'' those who would ''be my second self when I am gone'' (*Michael* 38–39). In ''The Thorn'' he achieved one of his greatest successes as a teacher of other poets.

Dorothy Wordsworth recorded in her Alfoxden Journal entry for 19 March 1798, a day otherwise distinguished apparently only by ''a severe hailstorm,'' that on that day ''William wrote some lines describing a stunted thorn'' (10). Those lines themselves almost bury the thorn from the beginning—

A toothless thorn with knotted joints;
Not higher than a two years child
It stands upon that spot so wild;
Of leaves it has repaired its loss
With heavy tufts of dark green moss,
Which from the ground in plenteous crop
Creep upward to its very top
To bury it for evermore.

(*PW* 2: 240n)

Of course Wordsworth's real intent with these lines and his later adaptations of them was to *prevent* the thorn from being buried—as he told Isabella Fenwick nearly half a century later: "I said to myself, 'Cannot I by some invention do as much to make this Thorn prominently an impressive object . . . ?' " (*PW* 2: 511, where "prominently" is printed "permanently," an error much repeated elsewhere).

This desire of the poet to keep the thorn *unburied* was not much shared by some of his most famous friends and contemporaries, with, however, one particularly notable, influential, and unexpected exception to be discussed later. Typical of many responses to Wordsworth's continuing efforts to make the thorn prominent and impressive were the critical remarks of Robert Southey, who in his 1798 article in *Critical Review* declared himself "altogether displeased" by the poem (200). Coleridge, though certainly not at first, denounced in later years, in *Biographia Literaria*, nearly half of that same poetic effort as "sudden and unpleasant sinkings" (*BL*, ed. Watson 195). For William Hazlitt, the thorn was weighed down not by its mosses but "with a heap of recollections," apparently a heap more than he could bear (11: 89). Writing in the *Edinburgh Review* in 1807,

Francis Jeffrey, acknowledging "pathos" and "a strong spirit of originality," found "The Thorn" nevertheless characterized by "occasional vulgarity, affectation, and silliness" (11: 214), and a year later returned to the attack with a parody of what he called Wordsworth's "very peculiar description" (12: 137). In *The Simpliciad*, one of several meager attempts in those years to revive the spirit of Pope's *Dunciad*, the author, who was apparently Bishop Richard Mant as Wordsworth said in a letter of later years (*LY* 5: 324), branded Wordsworth as "the founder of the simple school" and ridiculed specifically

> Poets, who fix their visionary sight
> On Sparrow's eggs in prospect of delight, . . .
> And dance with dancing laughing daffodills;
> Or measure muddy ponds from side to side,
> And find them three feet long and two feet wide.
>
> (cited in Havens 28)

And Byron—well, what Lord Byron did with "The Thorn" is a very special situation, one worthy of special attention hereafter.

But this is overstating the case, for Wordsworth's poem "The Thorn" has had also its admirers, and not just recent scholars and critics, some of whom have certainly lavished both attention and acclaim on it. (A sampling: Mary Jacobus discusses "The Thorn" as a radical and successful experiment in narrative method, in "communicating the incommunicable" [240–50]. John Jordan views the poem as "an exceedingly important moment" in Wordsworth's poetic development [*Why the LB?* 158]. Stephen Parrish's very convincing study of the dramatic merits of the poem calls it "a daring and skilful experiment in a new genre" [163].) But in the early years when the novelty of

"The Thorn" seemed particularly fresh, there was generally a bravado that accompanied any praise of the poem. Thus Thomas De Quincey, in a letter to Wordsworth dated 31 May 1803, expressed his exuberant "admiration and love for those delightful poems" (*Recollections* 385), of which "The Thorn" was one, but acknowledged "the abject condition of worldly opinion, in which Wordsworth then lived" (311) and the fact that "no applauding coterie ever gathered about him" (368). De Quincey later changed his views on Wordsworth, though not on the *Lyrical Ballads* nor "The Thorn." But in contrast to De Quincey's critical consistency, some of the very detractors cited above were also among the early enthusiasts for "The Thorn." Hazlitt, for example, recorded that when he *first* heard Coleridge read the poem, before Hazlitt even met Wordsworth,

> I felt that deeper power and pathos which have been since acknowledged, "In spite of pride, in erring reason's spite," as the characteristics of this author; and the sense of a new style and a new spirit in poetry came over me. It had something of the effect that arises from the turning up of the fresh soil, or of the first welcome breath of Spring, "While yet the trembling year is unconfirmed." (Woodring, *Prose* 289)

It is typical of admirers of "The Thorn," like Hazlitt, early and recent, to emphasize the *originality* of the poem. It was this originality, shared in various ways by many of the original *Lyrical Ballads*, that Southey disliked in his famous denunciation published in the *Critical Review* of October 1798: "The 'experiment,' we think, has failed" (204), and as for "The Thorn," its method of dramatic narration was particularly unpleasing: "He who personates tiresome loquacity, becomes tiresome himself" (200). At least Southey was, on this subject, consistent, for fourteen years later he was still telling De Quincey "that he considered Wordsworth's theory of poetic diction, and still more his principles as to the selection of subjects, and as to what constituted a poetic treatment, as founded in error" (De Quincey, *Recollections* 246).

Southey's great brother-in-law Coleridge lacked this consistency in his responses to "The Thorn." He was one of the most fervent, indeed most dogmatic, of the poem's early admirers. It was in its earliest years "an object of unqualified panegyric with him" (cited in Fruman 197). This fact we learn not from Coleridge, who was later to speak quite otherwise about "The Thorn," but from John Thelwall's marginal note on Coleridge's later negative comments on the poem in *Biographia Literaria*, a marginal note hidden in the recesses of the library at New York University until Norman Fruman discovered and published it. The better-known *public* statements of Coleridge on "The Thorn" all come from *Biographia Literaria*, especially Chapter 17, in which Coleridge gives the poem more attention, more detailed criticism, and a more general rejection of Wordsworth's aims and claims for it than he gives to any other work. "Had Mr. Wordsworth's poems," wrote Coleridge in the fourteenth chapter of *Biographia Literaria*, "been the silly, the childish things, which they were for a long time described as being; . . . they must have sunk at once, a dead weight, into the slough of oblivion." But instead, he said, those poems have long been treasured by people "of strong sensibility and meditative minds" (*BL*, ed. Shawcross 2: 7). Well—yes and no. But "The Thorn" at least has not fared particularly well with many readers, even many "of strong sensibility and meditative minds"—including, in fact, Coleridge, who (in Chapter 17) attacked nearly half of the poem as the sort of writing which "unprejudiced and unsophisticated hearts"—like his own, no doubt—can easily recognize as "sudden and unpleasant sinkings" (*BL*, ed. Shawcross 2: 37–38).

These "unpleasant sinkings," according to Coleridge, all amount to expressions of one of what he calls, in Chapter 22 of the *Biographia*, the characteristic defects of Wordsworth's poetry—namely "an undue predilection for the dramatic form," which, Coleridge claims, results inevitably in at least one of two "evils," either "an incongruity of style" or "a species of ventriloquism, where two are represented as talking while in truth one man only speaks" (*BL*, ed. Watson 258). Apparently Coleridge found both these evils in "The Thorn." He banished as incongruous the last two lines of the third stanza, the last seven of the tenth stanza, and all of stanzas 11 through 15 except for what he called "the four admirable lines at the commencement of the fourteenth" (*BL*, ed. Watson 197) (four acceptable lines out of a passage sixty-two lines long—this seems to take damning with faint praise to its extreme). Coleridge insisted, despite Wordsworth's claims to the contrary beginning with the "Advertisement" to the original volume of *Lyrical Ballads* in 1798, that "The Thorn" was a lyric poem, not a dramatic poem. However, Coleridge conceded that different rules could apply in a lyric poem, echoing Southey's criticism of nineteen years earlier: "It is not possible to imitate truly a dull and garrulous discourser without repeating the effects of dulness and garrulity" (*BL*, ed. Watson 194).

Coleridge's easy dismissal in 1817 of Wordsworth's dramatic claims for the poem is particularly striking in view of his obvious understanding and approval of those claims in 1798. John Thelwall's marginal note to this discussion in his copy of *Biographia Literaria* makes clear the contrast. Thelwall, not an admirer of "The Thorn," wrote, "I am amused with these concessions. Some years ago, when C[oleridge] & I had much talk about this poem in particular I could not wring from him any accordance with me upon the subject" (cited in Fruman 197). Wordsworth was totally convincing to Coleridge in 1798, totally unconvincing in 1817. If Coleridge was being pulled both ways for nearly two decades in a critical tug of war between Southey (and Thelwall and Jeffrey) on one side and Wordsworth on the other, clearly Southey's side eventually won him over. But it is odd to find Coleridge in such company in the *Biographia*, odd especially that it should be he who gave this final pronouncement against Wordsworth's supposed ventriloquism, odd to find in Coleridge's words such strong echoes from the hostile critics of past years (equally as hostile to Coleridge as to Wordsworth), like Jeffrey in the *Edinburgh Review* of April 1808, who wrote:

> In the story of "The Thorn," with all the attention we have been able to bestow, we have been utterly unable to detect any characteristic traits, either of a seaman, an annuitant, or a stranger in a country town. It is a style, on the contrary, which we should ascribe without hesitation to a certain poetical fraternity in the West of England, and which we verily believe, never was, and never will be, used by any one out of that fraternity. (137)

The fraternity to which Jeffrey assigned Coleridge as well as Wordsworth, and to which Coleridge had certainly belonged in the days of *Lyrical Ballads*—that fraternity Coleridge abandoned by the time he compiled *Biographia Literaria*. And not only did he abandon it, but he sided with those who all along had declared themselves its enemies. One can only wonder, and then wonder some more, at his motives. But it is hard to find any defect in "The Thorn" to justify the change in Coleridge's words and actions.

Coleridge was not the only one to change. Wordsworth himself made a number of revisions over the years in "The Thorn," both in the sections attacked by Coleridge and in the rest of the poem. Ernest de Selincourt claims that those revisions "were occasioned by Coleridge's criticism" rather than by Wordsworth's own growing poetic sense, but the claim is certainly questionable, at least in part, as is de Selincourt's insistence that most of the alterations are "unfortunate" (see his note in *PW* 2: 513). If Wordsworth deleted or changed some passages attacked by Coleridge, he also stuck to other attacked passages without change. And a number of his changes have nothing at all to do with Coleridge's comments. Whatever Coleridge's influence on the revisions, Wordsworth made his own changes for his own reasons, and they are consistent with his original aims. Thomas Hutchinson, in the notes to his 1920 edition of Wordsworth's poems, claims that the changes ruined the dramatic verisimilitude of "The Thorn." It is difficult to agree. Who can discern anything "unfortunate," for example, in the following change, with its elimination of what had been slightly silly feminine rhymes?

> 1798–1805:   It dried her body like a cinder,
> And almost turn'd her body to
> tinder.
>
> (131–32)

final version: A fire was kindled in her breast,
                  Which might not burn itself to rest.
                  (120–21)

Or this, with its similar increase in impact?

1798–1815:   Oh me! ten thousand times I'd
              rather
              That he had died, that cruel father!
              (142–43)

final version: O Guilty Father—would that death
                  Had saved him from that breach of
                  Faith!
                  (131–32)

Or this change, from tautology to striking description?

1798:   I've heard, the scarlet moss is red.
                 (221)

final version: I've heard, the moss is spotted red.
                  (210)

The fact is that Wordsworth's efforts in ''The Thorn'' have been, early and late, treated with a good deal of unjust disdain.

And yet art makes strange bedfellows—which brings us to the subject of Lord Byron's involvement with Wordsworth and his comments on ''The Thorn.'' Wordsworthians generally think of Byron, when they think of him at all, with some annoyance and regretful irony at his frequent unfriendly and unkind references to their poet in both his public poems and his private letters. As early as the 1809 publication of *English Bards and Scotch Reviewers*, Byron was aiming potshots at "vulgar Wordsworth" (903): "Let simple Wordsworth chime his childish verse" (917). Oddly enough, Byron put "the simple Wordsworth" in a school of poets directed by Southey, dismissing the leader to speak of his alleged disciple:

> Next comes the dull disciple of thy school,
> That mild apostate from poetic rule,
> The simple Wordsworth, framer of a lay
> As soft as evening in his favourite May,
> Who warns his friend "to shake off toil and
>   trouble,
> And quit his books, for fear of growing double";
> Who, both by precept and example, shows
> That prose is verse, and verse is merely prose;
> Convincing all, by demonstration plain,
> Poetic souls delight in prose insane;
> And Christmas stories tortured into rhyme
> Contain the essence of the true sublime.
>
> (235–46)

This may be, to some, quite witty, but it is certainly not accurate criticism. And such insults, even in fun, do not look like a very sound basis for much of a relationship between Byron and Wordsworth, either personal or artistic. But the truth is that both kinds of relationships developed between them. On their personal relationship, the news is recent, and we can thank the Dove Cottage Trust for the publication of Beth Darlington's edition of the Wordsworths' love letters. William wrote to Mary from London in 1812 about his meeting Byron there—"A Man who is now the rage in London, in consequence of his Late Poem Childe Haroldes pilgrimage" (147). Whatever personal relationship the two poets developed—and it was certainly brief—it included the cordial note of Lord Byron's franking Wordsworth's letters to save him the postage. And, in a similarly cordial vein, Wordsworth dismissed and forgave the insults of *English Bards and Scotch Reviewers*: "He wrote a satire some time since in which Coleridge and I were abused, but these are little thought of" (147). And if Wordsworth, upon reading *Childe Harold's Pilgrimage*, pronounced it "not destitute of merit; though ill-planned, and often unpleasing in the sentiments, and almost always perplexed in the construction" (160), he was only anticipating Byron's own objections to the same poem, raising a voice of critical candor at a time of nearly total adulation which Byron himself found excessive and ill founded.

If only Wordsworth could have foreseen what poetic achievements Byron's journey to Iberia, which by then had produced only the beginning of *Childe Harold's Pilgrimage*, would eventually produce! That is, the journey which Byron began in the summer of 1809, when Wordsworth's head too was full of Iberian matters following the Convention of Cintra. That journey laid the foundation for the great achievement of Byron's later poetic career, in which foundation Wordsworth's poem "The Thorn" would also have its importance.

That pilgrimage of 1809, three years before Wordsworth and Byron ever met but well after Byron had encountered, pondered, talked about, written about "The Thorn" and other early Wordsworth poems, was a daring thing, and hazardous, for the young poet to attempt. He journeyed from Lisbon across Portugal and Spain that summer, accompanied only by his friend

Hobhouse, the boy Robert Rushton, and their Portuguese guide named Sanguinetti—two foreign youths (Byron was only twenty-one), a boy, and a Portuguese guide with an Italian name racing across the Iberian Peninsula on horseback in time of war, with the threat of Napoleon's vast invading forces hanging over every town they passed through, with guerrilla warfare raging all around. Byron tried to make light of these conditions in a letter to his mother: "I had . . . every possible accommodation on the road, as an English nobleman in an English uniform is a very respectable personage in Spain at present" (*BLJ* 1: 219). But the hazards would not go away.

As the poet and his little group headed south for Seville, they came into the heavily fortified and rugged terrain of the Sierra Morena, where, as Hobhouse recorded, they were "passing over ground every inch of which had recently been fought over by French and Spaniards" (1: 10). The evidence of war excited Byron even as he reflected on the destruction yet to come. In *Childe Harold's Pilgrimage* he later wrote of these mixed feelings that the journey through the Sierra Morena inspired in him.

When the four travelers reached the mountain town of Monesterio, they made yet closer contact with the war and its participants. Hobhouse recorded that they "overtook two French prisoners and a Spanish spy on their way to Seville to be hanged." They became aware of guerrilla stragglers making their secret ways through these mountains, and they also had "contact with the Spanish troops" (1: 10).

Here, then, was a setting indeed for poetic inspiration—a setting exotic, dangerous, and beautiful. What could a Romantic imagination do in such a setting? It is well known what effects an Alpine or Welsh peak, a country churchyard, a Roman ruin, even the Elgin Marbles, could have on the English poetic mind. It seems a conscious deflation of the soaring balloon of Romantic imagination that Byron's only description in his letters of this spectacular setting was to call the Sierra Morena "a very sufficient mountain" (*BLJ* 1: 216). But "sufficient" is perhaps the right word after all, for the evidence is good that here in the Sierra Morena, on the road running south from Monesterio toward Seville, occurred the conception of the poet's masterpiece, *Don Juan*, which would begin to appear in print only a full ten years later and in whose technique Wordsworth and "The Thorn" were to be so greatly involved.

The evidence, of course, is that which Byron himself supplied in the prose Preface to *Don Juan* which was probably written in 1818. That Preface was withdrawn from publication along with the notoriously funny verse dedication of *Don Juan* to Southey when Byron and his publisher agreed to publish the first two cantos of the poem anonymously; consequently the Preface was never published till the twentieth century. The suppression of its publication surely must have cost Byron a pang, for the Preface wonderfully recreates the exotic setting of the Sierra Morena as if the poet had been there not longer ago than yesterday:

> The following epic Narrative is told by a Spanish Gentleman in a village in the Sierra Morena on the road between Monasterio & Seville—sitting at the door of a Posada with the Curate of the hamlet on his right hand a Segar in his mouth—a Jug of Malaga or perhaps, "right Sherris" before him on a small table containing the relics of an Olla Podrida—the time Sunset;—at some distance a

groupe of black eyed peasantry are dancing to the
sound of a flute of a Portuguese Servant belonging to two foreign travellers who have an hour
ago dismounted from their horses to spend the
night on their way to the Capital of Andalusia—
of these one is attending to the story—and the
other having sauntered further is watching the
beautiful movements of a tall peasant Girl whose
whole soul is in her eyes & her heart in the dance
of which she is the Magnet to ten thousand feelings that vibrate with her Own. Not far off a knot
of French prisoners are contending with each
other at the grated lattice of their temporary
confinement—for a view of the twilight festival—
the two foremost are a couple of hussars, one of
whom has a bandage on his forehead yet stained
with the blood of a Sabre cut received in the recent
skirmish which deprived him of his lawless
freedom;—his eyes sparkle in unison and his
fingers beat time against the bars of his prison to
the sound of the Fandango which is fleeting before
him.—Our friend the story-teller—at some
distance with a small elderly audience is supposed
to tell his story without being much moved by the
musical hilarity at the other end of the village-
Green.—The Reader is further requested to suppose him (to account for his knowledge of English)
either an Englishman settled in Spain—or a
Spaniard who travelled in England—perhaps one
of the Liberals who have subsequently been so
liberally rewarded by Ferdinand of grateful

memory—for his restoration. (References to Byron's Preface are to the ms. version printed in the Steffan and Pratt variorum, 2: 3–7.)

Probably nobody, not Merimee in *Carmen*, not Shaw in *Man and Superman*, has done better at conveying to us the power and poetry of the Sierra Morena than Byron in this prose Preface to *Don Juan*, the Preface he never even saw into print. But there are certainly many more questions raised by this Preface than answers given. How much is fact? Did *Don Juan* really begin to take shape in the poet's mind on that night of 24 July 1809? Did he really hear someone—an Englishman settled in Spain, or a Spaniard who had travelled in England, or himself talking aloud, or anybody else—tell tales of the legendary Don Juan, or of anybody, in the mountains that night? Did Sanguinetti in fact play the flute while black-eyed peasants danced and Hobhouse in fact watched one tall peasant girl with particular attention? Such questions perhaps violate the legitimate and necessary no-man's-land between fact and poetry.

But another question remains: Why did Byron go to such lengths to make this impressively evocative atmospheric Preface also a parody of Wordsworth's prefatory note to his poem "The Thorn?" Byron's own Preface begins:

In a note or preface (I forget which) by Mr. W. Wordsworth to a poem—the Subject of which as far as it is intelligible is the remorse of an unnatural mother for the destruction of her natural child—the courteous Reader is desired to extend his usual courtesy so far as to suppose that the narrative is narrated by "the Captain of a

Merchantman or small trading vessel lately retired upon a small annuity to some inland town—&c. &c.'' (3)

Parody, of course, can be either attack or praise; perhaps most often it is both at once. Byron's attacks were rarely restrained, and two paragraphs of this Preface express disgust at Wordsworth for abandoning "a mind capable of better things to the production of . . . trash," and at the "discerning British Public" for allowing Wordsworth to supersede Pope in its esteem. That the disagreement with Wordsworth was primarily political in its basis Byron freely admitted; the elder poet had lent his talents to the Tory cause—"purchased Talent" and "self-degradation" are typical terms of the denunciation.

Additionally, though, Byron also makes a point of linking the manner and method of *Don Juan* to that employed by Wordsworth in "The Thorn." "The Reader," writes Byron, "who has acquiesced in Mr. W. Wordsworth's supposition" about the narrator of his poem "is requested to suppose by a like exertion of Imagination" that the whole of *Don Juan* issues from the mouth of a gentleman narrator of undetermined nationality at sunset in the Sierra Morena. We are left to wonder: Is there parody of Wordsworth in all this? Yes, unquestionably. Is there disgust for talent that Byron thought wasted and sold-out? Yes, again. Is there also a strong element of laughter, particulary that kind of laughter that, as Byron put it in "Beppo," "Leaves us so doubly serious shortly after" (632)? Yes, of course. Is there anything else? Yes! It is this: Byron's *literary*, as distinct from personal and political, relationships with Wordsworth, and Wordsworth's importance for the English Romantic Movement and for the development of poetic and narrative art ever since.

The real issue, then, is this: Beyond parody, beyond disgust, beyond comedy, is there any serious artistic meaning and intent in Byron's invitation to readers of *Don Juan* to make "a like exertion of Imagination" as that required by Wordsworth for reading "The Thorn"? Is there a *serious* linkage between *Don Juan* and the Wordsworth of *Lyrical Ballads*?

We know how snide Byron could be on the subject of Wordsworth. Thomas Moore remembered Byron calling Wordsworth "that pedlar-praising son of a bitch" (*BLJ* 11: 198), and for one six-month period in 1820 and 1821 Byron almost never even mentioned the elder poet in his letters without calling him "Turdsworth" (*BLJ* 7: 158, 167, 168; 8: 66, 68), as, for example, when he wrote: "Of Turdsworth, the grand metaquizzical poet, / A man of vast merit, though few people know it" (*BLJ* 8: 68). But if this is snide and if Wordsworth is "Turdsworth," he is also, Byron says, "a man of vast merit." Just as in the Preface to *Don Juan* Wordsworth is accused of producing trash, he is also observed to possess "a mind capable of better things." And if Byron wrote Moore in 1818 that Wordsworth was the *only* member of the poetic profession "whose coronation" as head of the poets of the day "I would oppose," it is also true that Wordsworth was the only likely nominee for that title (*BLJ* 6: 47). The truth is that Byron had very mixed feelings about Wordsworth. For all the numerous and often nasty gibes, in public as well as in private, and despite all the hardening of their supposedly opposing political positions in later years, there remained also in Byron an admiration for Wordsworth's abilities and for many of Wordsworth's writings.

When Byron recalled in his "Detached Thoughts" of 1821 that he had briefly dabbled as an anonymous reviewer in his youthful days, he wrote, "In 1807—in a Magazine called

'Monthly Literary Recreations' I reviewed Wordsworth's trash of that time" (*BLJ* 9: 42). That 1807 review itself is a brief and not particularly perceptive critique of Wordsworth's 1807 *Poems in Two Volumes*, that publication which contained such notable poems as "Ode to Duty," "Elegiac Stanzas: Suggested by . . . Peele Castle," numerous patriotic sonnets, and the great Intimations of Immortality Ode (which Byron's review totally ignored). But Byron the reviewer certainly did not dismiss Wordsworth's productions in 1807 as "trash." On the contrary this review in *Monthly Literary Recreations* is heavy with praise, though not only praise, for the elder poet. Wrote Byron:

> The volumes before us are by the author of Lyrical Ballads, a collection which has not undeservedly met with a considerable share of public applause. The characteristics of Mr. W.'s muse are simple and flowing, though occasionally inharmonious verse, strong, and sometimes irresistible appeals to the feelings, with unexceptionable sentiments. Though the present may not equal his former efforts, many of the poems possess a native elegance, natural and unaffected, totally devoid of the tinsel embellishments and abstract hyperboles of several cotemporary [*sic*] sonneteers. (65)

And Byron cites passages from Wordsworth to demonstrate, as he says, that "the force and expression is that of a genuine poet" (65).

Already Byron was displaying in this early review that mingling of admiration and disappointment which would always characterize his feelings on Wordsworth. "When Mr. W.," he wrote, "ceases to please, it is by 'abandoning' his mind to the most common-place ideas, at the same time clothing them in language not simple, but puerile" (66). Probably Wordsworth's dearest friends and most devoted admirers would agree with Byron's critical judgment here. Yet even this comment, the most negative idea expressed in Byron's 1807 review, implies in Wordsworth an ability to please the critic most of the time, a poetic genius even when it is, as Byron puts it, "a genius worthy of higher pursuits" (66).

In the only approach to a mention of "The Thorn" in this review, that is, Byron's reference to *Lyrical Ballads*, presumably including "The Thorn," as "a collection which has not undeservedly met with a considerable share of public applause," there is none of the negative criticism that was to come, or that seemed to come, later in the Preface to *Don Juan*. In 1807, Byron found these early poems of Wordsworth, including "The Thorn," possessed of "a native elegance," a naturalness, a welcome lack of false ornament. In the 1818 Preface to *Don Juan*, however, Byron found, or said he found, "The Thorn" unpoetic and unintelligible. There is more to these differing judgments than changes in taste or even than growing awareness of supposed political differences.

There are, indeed, numerous positive comments on Wordsworth by Byron over the years. They are sprinkled among, often coupled with, the negative comments to convey above all Byron's ambivalence—not merely the hostility we usually think of, but the almost constant ambivalence—on the subject of his great contemporary. He was much aware of their contemporaneity. To John Murray he wrote in 1817 of his sense of "*all* of us—Scott—Southey—Wordsworth—Moore—Campbell—I" (*BLJ* 5: 265). To the same Murray he wrote that same year of ''Wordsworth more admired than read'' (*BLJ* 5: 252), a comment surely suggesting his own admiration. To James Hogg, Byron wrote, ''Wordsworth—stupendous genius! damned fool! These poets run about their ponds though they cannot fish. I am told there is not one who can angle—damned fools'' (*BLJ* 5: 13). Again, more damning. But Byron was never one to stay long determined to value a poet's fishing ability above his poetic ability, and after we consider briefly and discard easily the negative judgment of the lake poet's discipleship of Isaak Walton, we are left with the rest of Byron's judgment: ''Wordsworth—stupendous genius!'' To Leigh Hunt, Byron complained of his sense of Wordsworth's ''promise which is unfulfilled,'' of his great capacity as a poet, his ''much natural talent,'' ''the ability which lurks within him.'' And Byron again specifically made an exception of *Lyrical Ballads* and ''The Thorn'' as *not* belonging among the works of unfulfilled promise (*BLJ* 4: 324). In another letter to Hunt, Byron conceded, ''I do allow him [Wordsworth] to be 'prince of the bards of his time' upon the judgment of those who must judge more impartially than I probably do'' (*BLJ* 4: 317). To Murray, Byron had yet earlier written expressing some reservations, still widely shared among Wordsworth's readers, about the huge and recently published poem *The Excursion*: ''There must be many 'fine things' in Wordsworth,'' he wrote, ''—but I should think it difficult to make 6 quartos . . . all fine.'' And yet, fitting *The Excursion* into the whole of Wordsworth's production, Byron observed: ''There can be no doubt of his powers to do about anything'' (*BLJ* 4: 167). In short, as Leslie Marchand has accurately summarized, when Byron ''was not immediately irritated by provocation or controversy, he could pronounce balanced'' and indeed sincerely appreciative critical judgments on Wordsworth; the hostility we find so often in Byron's comments on Wordsworth is "by no means his most complete and genuine attitude" (*BLJ* 1: 15). And the easy dismissal in the Preface to *Don Juan* of Wordsworth's "The Thorn" is made highly questionable by Byron's contrary and much more numerous expressions elsewhere in praise and admiration for that poem and its companion pieces in the *Lyrical Ballads*.

Why then attack in 1818 in the Preface to *Don Juan* a poem that Byron, unlike Jeffrey, Southey, Coleridge, Hazlitt, and others by that time, really seems to have admired? The question can be answered in part by a closer examination of the details of the supposed attack. In an earlier and fragmentary version of his Preface, Byron claimed to have read "The Thorn" only "a few days ago" on the inside of his portmanteau where the paper on which Wordsworth's poem was printed had been used as lining by the manufacturer of the suitcase. Since the pages of the poem were glued to the inner surface of the suitcase, Byron had claimed not to be able to read or quote from the whole poem: "I tore away the page in attempting to turn it," he wrote (Steffan and Pratt 4: 5). In the final version of the Preface as Byron left it—the version which Willis Pratt correctly says shows "not only the importance Byron attached to it at the time of composition but also the care with which he partially prepared it for publication" (4: 5)—this fiction of the portmanteau lining was abandoned. Byron now claimed in his reference to Wordsworth to "quote from memory" (2: 3). But, curiously, whether quoting from a printed text or from memory, he quoted very badly. The poem of Wordsworth, never mentioned by its title, said Byron, "is that which begins with—'There is a thorn—it is so old' " (2: 3). Of course there is no such poem. Wordsworth's poem has a different opening line, crucially different: "There is a thorn;

it *looks* so old'' (Owen ed. of *Lyrical Ballads* 66; my emphasis). Byron's Preface then refers us to Wordsworth's note on the poem that requests the reader to imagine ''that the narrative is narrated by 'the Captain of a Merchantman or small trading vessel lately retired upon a small annuity to some inland town—&c. &c' '' (*DJ* Varioram 2: 3). But in the note to which our attention is called, Wordsworth, as Byron certainly knew, wrote something quite different about the narrator of ''The Thorn'':

> The character which I have here introduced speaking is sufficiently common. The Reader will perhaps have a general notion of it, if he has ever known a man, a Captain of a small trading vessel for example, who being past the middle age of life, had retired upon an annuity or small independent income to some village or country town of which he was not a native, or in which he had not been accustomed to live. Such men having little to do become credulous and talkative from indolence; and from the same cause, and other predisposing causes by which it is probable that such men may have been afflicted, they are prone to superstition. On which account it appeared to me proper to select a character like this to exhibit some of the general laws by which superstition acts upon the mind. (Owen ed. 139)

Observe. Not only is there no ''Merchantman'' here and no ''inland town'' (Wordsworth's poem in fact states the opposite; the narrator climbs the hill ''To view the ocean wide and bright'' [82]), there is not even a definite claim that the narrator is a retired seaman, but only that a retired seaman could serve as an example to convey a "general notion" of the type. There *is*, however, something of much greater significance to an understanding of Wordsworth's poem and purpose, and also Byron's poem and purpose. Clearly Wordsworth intended "The Thorn" to be not about a thorn tree and also not about what befell a young woman, pregnant and abandoned, and the child to whom she eventually gave birth; the poem, Wordsworth's note clearly informs us, is about the narrator. The poet asks us to attend primarily not to the story, which turns out to be full of deliberate contradictions and incompletenesses anyway, but to the *storyteller*. All of the *Lyrical Ballads*, Wordsworth wrote in his famous Preface to the 1800 edition of that collection, aimed at tracing "the primary laws of our nature" (*Prose* 1: 122). "The Thorn," one of the most important of the original *Lyrical Ballads*, was aimed, in this context, at exhibiting some of the general and primary laws of our nature "by which superstition acts on the mind." It does so by requiring us to keep our watchful eye on the narrator, the retired sea captain or whomever, the Wordsworthian ancient mariner. Yet Byron's Preface to *Don Juan* insists that "the Subject" of Wordsworth's poem "as far as it is intelligible is the remorse of an unnatural mother for the destruction of a natural child"—exactly what Wordsworth's note, to which Byron has called our attention, says is *not* the subject of the poem.

Byron, like all readers, could have his critical blind spots. He could also, like few men, be extraordinarily perceptive critically. Which was he being here? It seems certain that Byron wanted to turn a key for the reader of *Don Juan*, that his Preface to *Don Juan* was intended, beyond parody and facetiousness, to be *helpful* to readers entering his vast comic epic. Of course, he wrote to Moore from Venice in September 1818 that *Don Juan* was "meant to be a little quietly facetious upon every thing" (*BLJ* 6: 67). And truly the subject, in some sense, of his great poem is indeed "every thing." But there is a focal point moving across the vastness. *Don Juan* is not, in an organizational sense, a poem *about* everything, though it certainly includes a lot of things. Byron planned it as a poem, as Steffan writes, into "which he was to put as much as he dared of his thought and feeling about social men, and a great deal more than some people thought proper" (1: 8). But a poem cannot be structured around "every thing." And *Don Juan*, as everyone now realizes, is a highly structured poem. It is also surely not a poem about Juan himself, who is more often anti-hero than hero and who frequently seems not even a character or personality at all. If there is *one* thing the poem is about, it is the single word composed of the single letter which comes at the beginning of line one of the first canto: *I*. No need to wonder forever, as well we could and as some already have, whether this *I*, this narrator, is Byron himself, for the answer floats forever between yes and no. But that the poem is *about* its narrator, that the narrator is the unifying and structuring force of the poem, is clear. Juan we have more or less always with us, but many a reader feels positive relief when the narrator abandons his hero to go off in pursuit of some delicious digression, rejoicing that the poet did not really mean it when he threatened, "The regularity of my design / Forbids all wandering as the worst of sinning" (*DJ* 1.51–52). Other characters come and go in the poem. We welcome them. We delight in Donna Inez, Alfonso, Julia, Haidee, and so on right down to her frolic English grace Fitz-Fulke. But after they have strutted and fretted their hour upon Byron's stage and are then heard no more, we do not miss them. They are superb encounters; they are vivid creations, just as Wordsworth's Martha Ray is a vivid and unforgettable creation. But they are not really what the poem is about.

Both poems, *Don Juan* and "The Thorn," are *about* their narrators, and about the narrators' difficulties in narration. Whether Wordsworth's narrator was a retired sea captain or some other kind of man he never tells us, and for the poet's real purpose it does not matter at all. Whether Byron's narrator was an Englishman who spoke Spanish or a Spaniard who had traveled in England or a Byron who was neither of these is incidental, as the Preface to *Don Juan* makes plain. But in both poems the centrality of these narrator–characters is crucial.

Just what Wordsworth and Byron accomplish by putting their narrators in the center of their poems is only partially seen in the poems themselves. We are ever confronted by the truth that Wordsworth intentionally blurs the identity of the narrator and the facts of his tale and that, along with very similar kinds of intentional blurring and ambiguity, Byron's poem offers at least one additional difficulty, for *Don Juan* remains unfinished, a fragment. The purpose here then is not to try to make plain just what happened to Martha Ray, or her baby, or the townspeople, nor precisely how much the possible retired sea captain really knows and really tells. Nor is there any reason to try to summarize what Byron took over sixteen cantos to *begin*. The main intention here is to clarify and underscore that Byron planned to offer us help in his Preface for our reading of *Don Juan* and that much of that help consisted of a defense of Wordsworth's poem and of Wordsworth's dramatic method, and its lasting significance in "The Thorn"—a defense offered by Byron in despite, or perhaps because, of the then recent critical denunciation of poem and method in *Biographia Literaria*.

We have seen already how frequently the early nineteenth-century critics of "The Thorn," both those critics who loved the poem and those who denounced it, commented on Wordsworth's originality in structuring the poem. The primacy of what Byron called "our friend, the Story-teller," over the story was of course not an invention of English Romantic poets. A great deal of the meaning of Chaucer's *Canterbury Tales*, for example, lies in that poet's use of the same device. But as Byron began his work on *Don Juan*, he clearly realized that one of the most recent and most successful uses of the technique was Wordsworth's employment of it in several of the poems of the *Lyrical Ballads* but best of all in "The Thorn." If Wordsworth seemed to Byron capable of better work than much of what he had produced in 1818, he also seemed admirable in his own right as a creative genius and an innovator. Byron knew that "The Thorn," as he wrote in his 1807 review of Wordsworth for the magazine *Monthly Literary Recreations*, had "not undeservedly met with a considerable share of public applause" (65).

Needing then some way, and of course it had to be some witty way consistent with the hyperbolic and facetious tone of *Don Juan*, to call his readers' attention to the centrality of his own narrator, Byron hit fortunately on the opportunity to poke some fun at Wordsworth (again) and yet make use of and defend the Wordsworthian precedent. The poet of *Don Juan* could call attention to "The Thorn," could heap absurdly inaccurate and, to any careful reader, patently and intentionally unfair abuse on it. He could above all make a particular point of Wordsworth's note to his own poem and the importance in that poem of the narrator. And in an age that prized the imagination to the point of reverence, that tended to deify it by capitalization, Byron could drop in amid all the banter of his Preface to *Don Juan* the curiously serious-sounding recommendation that his readers approach his new poem "by a like exertion of Imagination" as that which Wordsworth had required for "The Thorn."

Even remembering those earlier antecedents already referred to, there is an immense and important freshness, originality, in this new look at narrative technique which Wordsworth and Byron insisted on our taking in "The Thorn" and *Don Juan*. Of course, many critics have noticed this originality, but not always with the accuracy that both Wordsworth and Byron demanded. W. H. Auden, for example, writes that "*Don Juan* is the most original poem in English; nothing like it had ever been written before" (xxiv). A striking judgment, all the more striking because it ignores Byron's urging readers to find "a like exertion of Imagination" in Wordsworth's poem. Similarly excited at the originality she thought she had found, Virginia Woolf, herself an important beneficiary of Wordsworth's setting literary minds in motion, wrote in her diary in 1918 of her first encounter with *Don Juan*; she was above all impressed by the narrative technique: "This method is a discovery by itself. It's what one has looked for in vain—an elastic shape which will hold whatever you choose to put into it." But she fails to credit any part of the discovery to Wordsworth, despite Byron's signal to do so. At least, unlike Auden, Virginia Woolf did link Wordsworth and Byron in her own thoughts—she says so. And she certainly admired what she found in such writing:

> I maintain that these illicit kinds of books are far more interesting than the proper books which respect illusions devoutly all the time. Still, it doesn't seem an easy example to follow;

and indeed like all free and easy things, only
the skilled and mature really bring them off
successfully.   (3–4)

These twentieth-century discoveries of the seeming originality
of the reflective narrative technique of "The Thorn" and
Don Juan are not really new, of course. William Hazlitt's parallel
comment on *Don Juan* was published in *The Spirit of the Age* in
1825: *Don Juan*, he accurately wrote (but without mentioning its
link to Wordsworth's poem, and, of course, without the benefit
of Byron's then unpublished Preface), "is . . . a poem written
about itself" (11: 75). This famous remark goes to the heart of
both *Don Juan* and "The Thorn," for both are poems about
poetry, about *telling*. This reflective and introspective technique
is both novel and immensely important, is, in fact, genuinely
revolutionary as part of the reorientation which is at the core
of the Romantic movement and of its lasting effects.

Such, then, is the importance of Wordsworth's experiment
in "The Thorn"—a new and lastingly significant way of examining the dramatic *inner* workings of narration and narrators. It
was too important a literary view, as Byron sensed, to be lost
amid the blindness of the traditional critics of Wordsworth's own
day or the even less responsible assaults of others who could
and should have recognized its value. And so we have Byron's
doubly ironic rescue mission of Wordsworth's achievement,
announced in the Preface to *Don Juan* and exemplified throughout
the poem. "When Wordsworth's understood," writes Byron
there, "I can't help putting in my claim to praise" (*DJ* 1.222.5–6).

One final, and additionally ironic, curiosity: Wordsworth
wrote Crabb Robinson in the winter of 1820, when Byron's newly
appearing mock epic was causing a great sensation, "I am

persuaded that Don Juan will do more harm to the English character, than anything of our time" (*MY* 3: 579). With this appraisal no doubt Byron himself would have agreed—and would have insisted, as he had already acknowledged privately, that such poetic subversion was just what he wanted, just what English poetry and narrative art could best use, and, further, that both the revolutionary poetic intent and the narrative technique underlying it he learned from "The Thorn."

CHAPTER EIGHT

"He Treated the Human Mind Well, and with an Absolute Trust"

Lost
Amid the moving pageant, I was smitten
Abruptly, with the view (a sight not rare)
Of a blind Beggar, who, with upright face,
Stood, propped against a wall, upon his chest
Wearing a written paper, to explain
His story, whence he came, and who he was.
Caught by the spectacle my mind turned round
As with the might of waters; an apt type
This label seemed of the utmost we can know,
Both of ourselves and of the universe,
And, on the shape of that unmoving man
His steadfast face and sightless eyes, I gazed,
As if admonished from another world.
(1850 *Prelude* 7.636–49)

These famous lines on Wordsworth's encounter with a source
of knowledge on the mob-filled streets of London typically gain
a good deal of their power and effect by their placement. They
come but a few lines following the poet's portrait of another
London guide, the preacher, that *"*pretty Shepherd, pride of all
the plains"—including, no doubt, those ancient cities of the plain,
Sodom and Gomorrah—he who mingles vanity with insensitivity
and affected eloquence with insincere artifice, *"*To rule and guide
his captivated flock" (see 7.551–72). As Wordsworth sits in this
fraud's "holy church" (1805 7.546), he could well be hearing

among the borrowed oratorical ornaments employed by the preacher some of the New Testament warnings against ''blind guides'' (see Matt. 23.16 and Rom. 2.19) and blind leaders of the blind and lost (see Matt. 15.13). But, paradoxically, as *The Prelude* states, it is only when Wordsworth leaves the church building and frees himself from being part of the ''captivated flock'' of this haranguing trickster, that the poet can encounter his own true guide, a blind guide but a valuable one, who can seemingly convey the admonishment from another world.

Such paradoxes abound in Wordsworth's poetry. One of his most constant themes is the failure, or at least the unreliability, of professional guides or of leaders for whom we might well have expectations of dependability. And, by contrast, genuine guidance abounds in his poetry, but often from unexpected sources. It is worthwhile to examine and compare some of these guides, both the failures and the successes, for insights into the poet's own claims as a poet–guide. Examining them will help us to understand his views of the workings, the guiding, the turning round of the human mind and spirit, *how* they can be led, and toward what. It is an investigation which can lead far into such matters as Wordsworth's thinking on education, on politics, and on the reciprocal roles of readers and poets.

One fascinating clue to Wordsworth's views on guides appears in the work in which he most decidedly claims the role of guide for himself, his *Guide through the District of the Lakes*, which, he insists on the title page, is ''for the use of tourists and residents'' alike (*Prose* 2: 151). In the section entitled ''Description of the Scenery of the Lakes,'' he writes that the guidance which he intends, surely quite a different intent from that of most guidebooks either then or now, will, in some instances, communicate to the traveller, who has already seen the objects, new information; and will assist in giving to his recollections a more orderly arrangement than his own opportunities of observing may have permitted him to make; while it will be still more useful to the future traveller, by directing his attention at once to distinctions in things which, without such previous aid, a length of time only could enable him to discover. It is hoped, also, that this Essay may become generally serviceable, by leading to habits of more exact and considerate observation than, as far as the writer knows, have hitherto been applied to local scenery. (2: 170–71)

These are noteworthy aims. Wordsworth as guide will, he claims, offer new information to those already initiated. He will help in forming "a more orderly arrangement" for the memory. He will draw attention to subtle distinctions. He will lead to habits of precise and thoughtful observation. Quite clearly, then, the poet saw himself not so much as a guide to the Lakes but a guide to the human intellect, a guide to the operations of the mind. Both in his own guidebook and in his poetic discussions of guiding, this *educational* element is always uppermost in his plans.

Many of the most reliable guides mentioned in Wordsworth's poetry, unlike both the London preacher and the blind beggar, are not human but are either abstractions or elements of Nature. Nature herself, as announced in "Tintern Abbey," is "the nurse, / The guide, the guardian of my heart" (109–10); it is she who leads the young man to bound "like a roe . . . o'er the mountains'' (67–70), and it is she who evokes that condition in us all, parallel to the actions of God in the Garden of Eden, whose creative power involves control over breathing and sleeping and waking and loneliness and companionship and all that is required to produce a living soul (the allusion is to Genesis 2.7, 21). For, writes Wordsworth, Nature guides us to

> that serene and blessed mood,
> In which the affections gently lead us on,—
> Until, the breath of this corporeal frame
> And even the motion of our human blood
> Almost suspended, we are laid asleep
> In body, and become a living soul.
>
> (41–46)

And Nature functions further as a guide in what the poet sees as her intention ''Through all the years of this our life, to lead / From joy to joy'' (124–25). Moreover, as the next-to-last book of *The Prelude* affirms, it is the *guiding* power of Nature which actually consecrates the visible outward forms of things and by so doing both liberates and leads the human mind to its fullest growth. Wordsworth's announcement of his ''convictions'' of these facts is expressed entirely in terms of acknowledging the abilities of a trustworthy guide, and it is a richly significant announcement:

> About this time did I receive
> Convictions still more strong than heretofore,
> Not only that the inner frame is good,
> And graciously composed, but that, no less,
> Nature for all conditions wants not power

To consecrate, if we have eyes to see,
The outside of her creatures, and to breathe
Grandeur upon the very humblest face
Of human life. I felt that the array
Of act and circumstance, and visible form,
Is mainly to the pleasure of the mind
What passion makes them; that meanwhile the
    forms
Of Nature have a passion in themselves,
That intermingles with those works of man
To which she summons him; although the works
Be mean, have nothing lofty of their own;
And that the Genius of the Poet hence
May boldly take his way among mankind
Wherever Nature leads; that he hath stood
By Nature's side among the men of old,
And so shall stand for ever.

                         (13.279-99)

Not only general Nature but specific elements of Nature also appear in Wordsworth's poetry as reliable guides. One thinks of just the rivers which the poet cites as trustworthy leaders of his steps, and of the steps of common humanity. There is, for example, "the maddened Reuss our guide" in *Descriptive Sketches* (197), but in the same poem the "indignant waters of the infant Rhine" (163) and the gleaming waters of the Tusa (156-57) also lead him properly. The Tusa is mentioned in the Alpine travels of *Prelude* 6, too, where "our journey we renewed / Led by the stream" (649-50), in a context, again, of paradox to be considered later. And in *The Waggoner* even the poet's Muse has "murmuring Greta for her guide" (4.17). Two decades later, another river shows both poet and Muse the way in the River Duddon sonnets. Sonnet 12 of that sequence opens by urging the Muse to keep up with the river ("On, loitering Muse—the swift Stream chides us—on!") and a few lines later Wordsworth speaks of himself as "The Bard who walks with Duddon for his guide" (11). By the end of the sequence, in the graceful "After-thought," the poet is calling the river "my partner and my guide" (34.1), with a guidance which seems eternal: "Still glides the stream, and shall for ever glide; / The Form remains, the Function never dies" (5–6).

In addition to these leading rivers, other elements of Nature can be equally reliable guides for Wordsworth. One thinks of the pillar of cloud which led Moses and his people as they wandered in their wilderness. And one finds that same symbol for divine guidance evoked in the opening passage of *The Prelude* in the lines "and should the chosen guide / Be nothing better than a wandering cloud, / I cannot miss my way!" (1.16–19).

Even more important among the elements of Nature which lead well, according to Wordsworth, is light—guiding light. One thinks of the scriptural affirmation that "God is light" (1 Jn. 1.5) and sees evidence for the claim in many places in Wordsworth's poetry. It may be the light of a "kindling" sky of sunrise, as in the "dedicated Spirit" passage of *Prelude* 4 (320–37). It may be the light of a crucial star, like that which prevents a murder in *The Borderers*:

> Upward I cast my eyes, and, through a crevice,
> Beheld a star twinkling above my head,
> And, by the living God, I could not do it.
>
> (2.438–40)

Or, again with divine character, it may be the light cast by the polar star of which the Wanderer speaks in *The Excursion* as he traces the metaphysical guiding influences of the development of astronomical awareness in mankind:

> Chaldean Shepherds, ranging trackless fields,
> Beneath the concave of unclouded skies
> Spread like a sea, in boundless solitude,
> Looked on the polar star, as on a guide
> And guardian of their course, that never closed
> His stedfast eye.
>
> (4.694–99)

Or it may be the very divinity of light itself, the same Muse of epic light invoked previously by Milton and Spenser. This is Urania, the heavenly one, Muse of celestial light. As Spenser writes in lines which must surely have appealed to Wordsworth, in *The Teares of the Muses*, she is source of that knowledge by which we ''judge of Natures cunning operation'' and by which ''we do learne our selves to knowe, / And what to man, and what to God wee owe'' (501–04).

Like these great poets before him, Wordsworth expresses the desire not only to receive this light of heaven from what he identifies at one point as ''the primal source / Of all illumination'' (Prospectus to *The Excursion* 101–02, *PW* 5: 6), but also to *transmit* it. That is to say that, interested as the poet is in identifying possible guides, evaluating them, distinguishing the trustworthy from the unreliable, he is above all eager to imitate them, become a trusty guide himself, a light. His prayer is

> that my Song
> With star-like virtue in its place may shine

196

> Shedding benignant influence, and secure,
> Itself, from all malevolent effect
> Of those mutations that extend their sway
> Throughout the nether sphere!
>
> (Prospectus 88-93, *PW* 5: 6)

It is interesting though, even here, that Wordsworth is not quite *certain* of the reliability of the most seemingly trustworthy guides. Even in the moment of invoking Urania, he reveals a doubt, an ongoing interior debate:

> Urania, I shall need
> Thy guidance, or a greater Muse, if such
> Descend to earth or dwell in highest heaven!
>
> (Prospectus 25-27, *PW* 5: 3)

This is a striking expression to come from so determined a poet. In other manuscripts of the Prospectus, he identifies this same invoked deity as none other than "great God" (ms. 1), and "great God / Thou who art breath and being, way and guide" (ms. 2), and even "great God / Almighty being who art light and law" (ms. 3, *PW* 5: 6). What is striking is not that Wordsworth should appeal to his God for divine guidance in his poetry, nor even that he should call this deity by the pagan name Urania; for here he has Milton for a guide, the Milton who in *Paradise Lost* addresses Urania and then promptly adds, "The meaning, not the Name I call" (7.5). What is striking, and puzzling, is Wordsworth's calling on Urania, identifying her with God, describing her as "the primal source" of knowledge, and then abruptly suggesting that she may not after all be a good enough guide ("I shall need / Thy guidance, or a greater Muse") only to recoil a bit at that suggestion and to wonder aloud whether there *could* be a greater Muse. It is these seeming contradictions and confusions that I shall address in what follows.

To the list of reliable but nonhuman guides mentioned in Wordsworth's poetry, such things as Nature, rivers, clouds, light, could be added such abstractions as *hope*, as when the Wanderer in *The Excursion* prays

> To the virtuous grant
> The penetrating eye which can perceive
> In this blind world the guiding vein of hope.
> (6.256–58)

Or *love*, as when Dorothy writes in the poem "Loving and Liking," which her brother obviously approved of and published with his own works, "Our heavenward guide is holy love" (67).

But there are also trustworthy *human* guides, though in dealing with them we become almost instantly aware of the poetic ironies involved. To some of these human guides Wordsworth pays grateful tribute with no hint of reservation. There is Ann Tyson, for example, his old landlady at Hawkshead. When he returned there after nine months at Cambridge, he found that his relationship with the good old woman, and with the nurturing village which she represented, had actually deepened during the absence:

> My aged Dame
> Walked proudly at my side: she guided me;
> I willing, nay—nay, wishing to be led.
> —The face of every neighbor whom I met
> Was like a volume to me.
> (*Prelude* 4.64–68)

Similarly, both in early years and in retrospect, his headmaster at Hawkshead School, William Taylor, provided reliable guidance, as the poet acknowledges in telling of visiting the grave of Taylor some years after the latter's death:

> This faithful guide, speaking from his death-bed,
> Added no farewell to his parting counsel,
> But said to me, "My head will soon lie low"
> And when I saw the turf that covered him,
> After the lapse of full eight years, those words,
> With sound of voice and countenance of the Man,
> Came back upon me, so that some few tears
> Fell from me in my own despite. But now
> I thought, still traversing that widespread plain,
> With tender pleasure of the verses graven
> Upon his tombstone, whispering to myself:
> He loved the Poets, and, if now alive,
> Would have loved me, as one not destitute
> Of promise, nor belying the kind hope
> That he had formed, when I, at his command,
> Began to spin, with toil, my earliest songs.
>
> (*Prelude* 10.537–52)

Not surprisingly, some of the most frequently mentioned human guides in Wordsworth's poetry are other poets. The "Extempore Effusion" occasioned by the death of James Hogg explicitly mentions as reliable sources of guidance not only Hogg— "The Ettrick Shepherd was my guide" (4)—but Walter Scott— "My steps the border-minstrel led" (8)—and, by implication, includes such other poetic friends and guides as Charles Lamb and, of course, Coleridge, "The rapt One, of the godlike forehead, / The heaven-eyed creature" (17–18). Robert Burns is singled out as a worthy guide too, at least to his sons, and at least in some matters: "His judgment with benignant ray / Shall guide, his fancy cheer, your way," but with a pointed warning about too great a reliance on a guide whose path Wordsworth found not always trustworthy:

> But ne'er to a seductive lay
> Let faith be given;
> Nor deem that "light which leads astray,
> Is light from Heaven."
> ("To the Sons of Burns," 39–42)

And, even more expectably, there are the tributes to older poets, like the acknowledgment in *The Prelude* that Wordsworth could consider becoming a guide himself in a lost and drowning world when he stopped to contemplate his own debt to some of his great predecessors:

> Oftentimes at least
> Me hath such strong entrancement overcome,
> When I had held a volume in my hand,
> Poor earthly casket of immortal verse,
> Shakespeare, or Milton, labourers divine!
> (5.161–65)

Books and those who write them, he tells us, constitute, along with "common intercourse with life," what the poet somewhat evasively calls a "Guide faithful as is needed" (11.95–99). Poets and their books, then, can be, and often are, light from heaven. But human guides are not infallible, and poets, even the same revered poets, can also send forth a light that leads astray. Wordsworth at once champions the guidance of books and questions their possible motives and condemns their fallacies:

> Deeply did I feel
> How we mislead each other; above all,
> How books mislead us, seeking their reward
> From judgments of the wealthy Few, who see
> By artificial lights; how they debase
> The Many for the pleasure of those Few;
> Effeminately level down the truth
> To certain general notions, for the sake
> Of being understood at once, or else
> Through want of better knowledge in the heads
> That framed them; flattering self-conceit with
>   words,
> That, while they most ambitiously set forth
> Extrinsic differences, the outward marks
> Whereby society has parted man
> From man, neglect the universal heart.
>
> (13.206–20)

There is a deeper question in all this. Wordsworth's characteristic reverence for human nature and the human mind does not blind him to the fact that human nature is full of inconsistency and that "the universal heart" of mankind can at times beat variously and unreliably. His account of his opening days at Cambridge can in fact stand as a rather accurate summation of his lifelong experiences with the confusion offered by the conflicting claims of human guides: "Questions, directions, warnings and advice, / Flowed in upon me from all sides" (3.23–24).

One who avidly and unguardedly seeks guidance from all who claim to give it can become, paradoxically, at once both informed and ignorant. Such is the case of the model schoolboy described in *Prelude* 5. The egotism of his human guides combines with his own willingness to be misled to produce a monster. Educated in an infinity of human trivialities, he becomes subhuman. Unwittingly, such a child is the victim of those whom Wordsworth denounces for their abuses as "the keepers of our time, / The guides and wardens of our faculties" (353–54), whose functions are "control" and confinement and "presumption" (355–58). And the boy who has ignorantly trusted in *all* ingredients of human nature is despoiled, by his guides, of his own naturalness:

> Full early trained to worship seemliness,
> This model of a child is never known
> To mix in quarrels; that were far beneath
> His dignity; with gifts he bubbles o'er
> As generous as a fountain; selfishness
> May not come near him, nor the little throng
> Of flitting pleasures tempt him from his path;
> The wandering beggars propagate his name,
> Dumb creatures find him tender as a nun,
> And natural or supernatural fear,
> Unless it leap upon him in a dream,
> Touches him not. To enhance the wonder, see
> How arch his notices, now nice his sense
> Of the ridiculous; nor blind is he
> To the broad follies of the licensed world,
> Yet innocent himself withal, though shrewd,
> And can read lectures upon innocence;

A miracle of scientific lore,
Ships he can guide across the pathless sea,
And tell you all their cunning; he can read
The inside of the earth, and spell the stars;
He knows the policies of foreign lands;
Can string you names of districts, cities, towns,
The whole world over, tight as beads of dew
Upon a gossamer thread; he sifts, he weighs;
All things are put to question; he must live
Knowing that he grows wiser every day
Or else not live at all, and seeing too
Each little drop of wisdom as it falls
Into the dimpling cistern of his heart:
For this unnatural growth the trainer blame,
Pity the tree.—Poor human vanity,
Wert thou extinguished, little would be left
Which he could truly love; but how escape?
For, ever as a thought of purer birth
Rises to lead him toward a better clime,
Some intermeddler still is on the watch
To drive him back, and pound him, like a stray,
Within the pinfold of his own conceit.

                                    (5.298–336)

It is in this awareness of the fallibility of human guides that
Wordsworth makes some of his most telling observations on how
our minds function, how we can be led astray, and how we must
develop a genuine and trustworthy sense of discernment. The
experience he recounts of crossing the Alps, for example, is
instructive, particularly in its revised form. In the 1805 version
of *Prelude* 6, the young Wordsworth and Robert Jones are

said to have encountered by chance "a band / Of travellers" (1805 6.494–95), and these the two young Britons abroad made their "guides" (497). Only in a very late revision of *The Prelude* did these "guides" become "our guide" (1850 6.565), a single person sounding in fact like someone hired to show them the way. The change is significant, for it underlines one of the things Wordsworth wants to stress about guides—namely, don't put blind trust in a professional. This one guide of the 1850 version abandons his charges as they eat their lunch, and he is never seen again. Without him they follow what seems the obvious path, but it leads them astray. Lost and frustrated, they are rescued "by fortunate chance" (577) when they encounter a stray peasant who can tell them where the right road lies but cannot save them from disappointment.

There are very similar incidents with guides scattered throughout *The Prelude*. Sometimes, as in the 1850 version of crossing the Alps, they actually involve a literal guide who fails to guide. Thus, in the famous section explaining "spots of time" in *The Prelude*, the whole experience of the five-year-old boy's encounter with the "visionary dreariness" of the ancient place of execution occurs because of a guide that fails. Wordsworth pointedly speaks of this person, identified in the 1799 and 1805 tellings as "honest James," in terms ultimately of absolute oxymoron: he is at first "my encourager and guide" (12.230), but he becomes simply "my lost guide" (12.257), *so* lost a guide that he never reappears in the narrative. Of course, this experience was vitally important for the poet and for the development of his epistemology, so much so that it led him to exclaim over the significance of being unguided, lost:

Oh! mystery of man, from what a depth
Proceed thy honours. I am lost, but

> See in simple childhood something of the base
> On which thy greatness stands.
>
> (12.272–75)

Wordsworth makes no great point here of casting blame or responsibility on "honest James," though it is easy to imagine that if any physical disaster had overtaken the child, a child on horseback and so young that his "inexperienced hand / Could scarcely hold a bridle" (12.226–27), the lost guide would have had to answer for it. There is, in fact, in this narration the contrary hint that a lost guide may be the best kind, at least sometimes. For a vision of "the hiding places of man's power" (12.279) to be opened, the visionary being must be at least somewhat self-sufficient. Still speaking of man's greatness, Wordsworth adds, "But this I feel, / That from thy self it comes, that thou must give, / Else never canst receive" (12.275–77).

Certainly, some of these same ideas are present in the culminating description of the climbing of Mt. Snowdon given in the final book of *The Prelude*. Once again we have a trained guide, a professional, "the shepherd who attends / The adventurous stranger's steps, a trusty guide" (14.8–9). In the 1805 version, this guide is actually said to receive his authority by inheritance, almost like a hereditary monarch of the mountain, for "by ancient right / Of office" he serves as "the stranger's usual guide" (13.7–8). As Wordsworth and Jones begin their ascent in the breezeless fog, the guide fulfills his duty properly enough; he is their "conductor" (14.17). But somewhere in the mist the roles become reversed, and when the moment of discovery comes, when "instantly a light upon the turf / Fell like a flash" (14.39–40), no guide is there to point it out. Instead the poet has somehow become, "as chanced, the foremost of the band'' (14.34). In terms of realistic narration, of course, as any-one knows who has climbed a mountain with other people, it is easy and natural for the climbers to get out of their original positions. But Wordsworth here is certainly doing more than tell-ing the story of a mountain climb. And one of the things he is saying is that a journey of discovery may well start out as a guided tour but must inevitably end up in solitary vision.

In two other examples of lost guides in *The Prelude*, Wordsworth is careful to give detailed explanation of why the guide is ultimately unsuccessful. One of these lost guides is William Godwin, who of course represents all prophets of what Wordsworth comes to consider a narrow rationalism, all guides who lead by only one kind of light. The poet regrets the willingness of such a guide to narrow his focus to such a degree that Nature is denied. But the failure of this guide is due not only to the nar-row vision of the *guide* but also to the willingness, even eager-ness, of the *guided* to be duped. The false leader's appeal is, as with the miseducated schoolboy in *Prelude* 5, to the ego, the pride, of the led and also to that desire which is always so prominent in human affairs, the desire to oversimplify, to find one lost chord and play it endlessly to the exclusion of all other tones. Godwinism was accepted for a guide briefly, ''Found ready welcome,'' as Wordsworth says (11.228), because it seemed so flattering and so simple:

> The dream
> Flattered the young, pleased with extremes, nor least
> With that which makes our Reason's naked self
> The object of its fervour. What delight!
> How glorious! in self-knowledge and self-rule,

>To look through all the frailties of the world,
>And, with a resolute mastery shaking off
>Infirmities of nature, time, and place,
>Build social upon personal Liberty,
>Which, to the blind restraints of general laws
>Superior, magisterially adopts
>One guide, the light of circumstances, flashed
>Upon an independent intellect.
>
>(11.232–44)

That is, the very narrowness and oversimplification which doomed Godwinism to be a failed system of guidance was that which led to its easy initial acceptance. The truth is shown here by a reversal: a successful guide is one who accepts and encourages both alertness and independence in the followers, followers who are, in the phrase Wordsworth came to understand at the end of *The Prelude*, "ever on the watch, / Willing to work and to be wrought upon" (14.102–03).

The last instance of failed guides from *The Prelude* to be discussed here is of quite a different sort from these others. When Wordsworth first meets this guide, he decides "To cleave unto this man" (5.116). In a world of nearly constant misleading, where "we mislead each other" and "books mislead us" (13.207–08), the poet accepts this man, along with the book he personifies, as "a guide / . . . who with unerring skill / Would through the desert lead me" (5.81–83). This trustworthy guide, of course, is the combination Arab–Quixote of the dream vision of Book 5. There seems no danger in putting complete trust in such a guide. And yet, Wordsworth says, when "I called after him aloud" (5.133), it was in vain; "he heeded not" (5.134), and finally the guide vanishes altogether, leaving the poet "in terror" (5.138).

Clearly the problem in guidance here is not with the guide of "unerring skill" but with the guided, the follower. Essential to successful guidance is a follower who can keep up, who possesses sufficient strength and perhaps courage to stay with his leader. Wordsworth expresses for this guide a profound "Reverence . . . to a being thus employed" (5.150), but he rightly and humbly acknowledges himself unequal to the task of following the unique trail of the mighty Cervantes. The point is important: for valid, successful guiding to take place there must be both a guide of unerring skill, a hard enough thing to find in human terms, and also a follower who combines independence with determination and undaunted fortitude. Such human combinations are rare indeed, and thus they are all the more to be prized when achieved.

Much more common, inevitably, than such successful instances of leadership, and followership, are the numerous occasions in human history of failed guidance. Perhaps surprisingly, in Wordsworth, even Nature can fail as a guide. So much depends on the motives of the one who would be led. Thus, the Solitary, in *Excursion* 3, speaks of the failure of Nature to guide him aright, while acknowledging that the failure was actually his:

> Here Nature was my guide,
> The Nature of the dissolute; but thee,
> O fostering Nature! I rejected—smiled
> At others' tears in pity; and in scorn
> At those which thy soft influence sometimes
> drew
> From my unguarded heart.
>
> (807–12)

And similarly, books failed the Solitary too, including, as he says, *the* book of guidance, the Bible, though again he confesses the fault in himself rather than in the guide, though he sees that fault as caused by Nature:

> Within the cabin stood
> That volume—as compass for the soul—
> Revered among the nations. I implored
> Its guidance; but the infallible support
> Of faith was wanting. Tell me, why refused
> To One by storms annoyed and adverse winds;
> Perplexed with currents; of his weakness sick;
> Of vain endeavours tired; and by his own,
> And by his nature's, ignorance, dismayed!
>   (3.861–69)

For both the Solitary and Wordsworth, perhaps the most disappointing experiences with failed guides are their encounters with political theorists and the military leaders who so often assume the responsibility of implementing the notions of those theorists. The Solitary dismisses these kinds of guides as representing, when strong, "a power / Formal, and odious, and contemptible" (3.825–26), or, when puny, a condition in which "The weak are praised, rewarded, and advanced" (3.828). In neither kind of situation is reliable guidance to be found. This is the general truth insisted on by Wordsworth in his considerations of political guides. But these considerations were for him a lifelong concern, and he repeatedly found himself engaged in specific studies of political claims to reliable guidance.

One of the most detailed of Wordsworth's considerations in his poetry of the matter of political and military leadership appears in the series of sonnets which he wrote in response to the Iberian crises of the first decade of the nineteenth century. These poems, though neglected by critics, offer rich insights into the poet's complex views on the nature of a reliable guide and the requirements for the trustworthy follower. The circumstances out of which these sonnets were produced are almost as important for understanding Wordsworth's thinking on principles of leadership as what the poems themselves express, and they require a brief digression to fill in some of that background.

"William . . . has written 15 fine political sonnets," writes Dorothy to Catherine Clarkson at the end of December 1810 (*MY* 2: 460). The poet himself had written Francis Wrangham twenty-one months before that "verses" had been "out of my head for some time" (*MY* 2: 312), so Dorothy's announcement of the political sonnets seems to suggest her brother's returning to composition after what could have seemed to his friends an unusual hiatus in his poetic activity. In fact, however, Wordsworth was busy. Popular uprisings against Napoleon's imposed rule in Spain and Portugal had begun in 1807. The insurgents' early successes had won them many allies among Bonaparte's enemies; and the English government, urged on by considerations of military strategy and need as well as by idealistic appeals of men like Richard Brinsley Sheridan, who advocated in Parliament "the rescue of a nation's liberty" (Ward and Gooch 3: 368), formed an alliance with the Iberian rebels. But shortly, in the view of many, the British generals in command of these allied forces betrayed the Portuguese and Spanish by signing with the French near Lisbon the so-called Convention of Cintra, giving Napoleon's defeated troops a free ride home in British ships, without requiring guarantees against future invasions and without restrictions on plunder.

"Never did any public event cause in my mind so much sorrow as the Convention of Cintra, both on account of the Spaniards and Portuguese, and on our own," writes the poet in February 1809 to Daniel Stuart, editor of the London *Courier* (*MY* 2: 288). More than sorrow there was thought, the kind of thought that Wordsworth had had back in the days of the French Revolution, when he pondered theories of guidance and, as he says in *The Prelude*,

> began
> To meditate with ardour on the rule
> And management of nations; what it is
> And ought to be; and strove to learn how far
> Their power or weakness, wealth or poverty,
> Their happiness or misery, depends
> Upon their laws, and fashion of the State.
>
> (11.98–104)

Now, two decades later, the ardent meditation continues, still focused on principles of national guidance and leadership but with a different locale: "His first and his last thoughts are of Spain and Portugal," writes Dorothy (*MY* 2: 280–81).

Perhaps the most significant result of this meditation on Iberian politics and wars is Wordsworth's longest single work, the prose tract *Concerning . . . the Convention of Cintra*. But the poet's meditations and his following with great involvement the unfolding of events in Spain and Portugal did not end with the tract—hence the series of "fine political sonnets" announced by Dorothy nearly two years after the tract was written. Her calling them fifteen sonnets has occasioned some confusion, for it is not easy to identify exactly which fifteen poems she means. Between them, Mary Moorman and Mark Reed point to twenty possible candidates for the fifteen "fine" sonnets, all written during this time of deepening crisis in Iberian military affairs and parallel crisis in national leadership and guidance in England, and all published in Wordsworth's two-volume *Poems* of 1815. (See *MY* 2: 460 and Reed 410–11; Reed notes that "the evidence is not very strong" for deciding exactly which poems Dorothy had in mind. I shall refer to the sonnets by the numbers given them in Part II of "Poems Dedicated to National Independence and Liberty" in *PW* 3.)

Dorothy's letter to Catherine Clarkson at the end of 1810 notes that the sonnets deal with "The King of Sweden, Buonaparte, and the struggles of the Peninsula" (*MY* 2: 460). In fact, of the twenty sonnets suggested by Moorman and Reed, only one (sonnet XX) deals with the dethroned King Gustavus IV of Sweden, whom the poet chooses as exemplifying a righteous and trustworthy guide to his nation, in contrast with Napoleon. Two other sonnets deal with Austrian and German resistance to the French Emperor (sonnets XVIII and XIX). Another two discuss the character of the Emperor himself and point to principles for resisting and defeating him (sonnets XXI and XXXIII). The other fifteen sonnets, those to be discussed more fully here, deal with Spain and Portugal—more accurately, with Spain, for the words *Portugal* and *Portuguese* never appear in any of Wordsworth's poems. He had, like many another armchair traveller not be bothered with foreign distinctions, already amalgamated the two nations in his mind. And anyway, his aim was a discussion of principles of political guidance, not contemporary political description. In the *Cintra* tract he had written: "I have indeed spoken rather of the Spaniards than of the Portuguese; but what has been said, will be understood as applying in the main to the whole Peninsula. The wrongs of the two nations have been equal, and their cause is the same: they must stand or fall together" (229). (Even Lord Byron, whose travels in Iberia were not by armchair, used the word *Portugal* only once in all his poetry, and then only to equate it with Spain: "In Spain . . . much the same in Portugal" [*DJ* 3.683–84].)

Dorothy's same 1810 letter also suggests a reason why none of the Iberian sonnets was published until 1815, the year of Waterloo. She and Mary in 1810 were encouraging their publication in the *Courier,* the same London paper which had earlier carried parts of the *Cintra* tract, "both in order that they might be read," she writes, "and that we might have a little profit from his industry." But her brother was apparently resisting all notions of publication, and Dorothy hints that he was depressed and disgusted over the alarming absence from the political scene of any trustworthy guides and over the dreary prospects for genuinely high-principled success in the military activity and leadership in the Peninsula—"heartless respecting Wellington's doing much" is Dorothy's phrase. For a time, the poet, though busy in composition, ceased to be "a man speaking to men." Dorothy reports his disillusionment "with critics, Readers, newspaper-Readers—and the talking public" (*MY* 2: 460).

Interestingly, several later critics have insisted that it was this Iberian crisis which produced a new and, for Wordsworth, essentially apostate theory of guides and guidance. It is at this period, according to one such critic, that Wordsworth, in his great alarm over the growing success of Napoleon's malevolent leadership, developed and "enunciated an anti-democratic doctrine which foreshadows the 'hero-worship' of Carlyle" (Baugh 1145). Another critic points to what he calls Wordsworth's "conservative . . . idea of great men" as reliable guides in political affairs

(Lehman, "Doctrine" 640), in which the very qualities of Carlyle's worshipped hero are to be seen in Wordsworth's treatment of "the actions of heroes, statesmen, legislators, and warriors" (Lehman, *Theory* 54). Sixteen years earlier, the poet had written to his friend William Matthews of his disgust for "the infatuation profligacy and extravagance of men in power" (*EY* 124). If then the Iberian sonnets of 1810 do represent a new view of political leadership, it would be all the more important for us to take a hard look at these poems. But we shall find, in fact, that Wordsworth here remains consistent in his caution regarding human guides and his insistence on limiting the role and scope of any political guide.

Certainly there are guides and heroes in these poems. When Carl Woodring remarks that Wordsworth as "political sonneteer watched for peoples and their heroes to celebrate" (123), he states a truth, but it is a truth which might be easily misunderstood. If Wordsworth is not exactly worshipful, his attitude is certainly one of admiration for those who fill "from morn to night the heroic scene / With deeds of hope and everlasting praise," as he writes in sonnet XXII (9–10). But what does the poet mean by "heroic"? Who are these guides and heroes, these "captains" and "chiefs" (31.5–6)? They fall into two categories, the same two categories named in the section in *The Prelude* on the poet's observations on guides and guidance during the French Revolution—"The noble Living and the noble Dead" (11.394). The noble Dead of the Iberian sonnets are individuals; they have names like Sertorius, the Roman general who fought against Senatorial tyranny and whose followers from Roman Spain, according to Plutarch, settled as tenacious defenders of freedom in the Canary Islands—the same Sertorius whose heroism along with his "Friends / And Followers" so impressed

Wordsworth that he relates in *The Prelude* how he considered making them the subject of a major poem (1.190 ff.); or like Viriathus, the pre-Christian shepherd who led the rebellious Lusitanians in their fight against Roman domination (see sonnet XXXI). But the noble Living of Iberia in 1810 are of a different sort and offer a downright democratic sort of guidance. There are the anonymous members of "roving Spanish Bands" (30.5); they are the "Spaniards of every rank" (29.10), the mingled "Peasant and lord" (26.13), nameless defenders of home and family and liberty. There are the true heroes of the Iberian struggle against Napoleon, representatives of popular power and right. Wordsworth, by a rather complex allusion in sonnet XXXI, compares them to Milton's angels in the War in Heaven, "the least of whom," according to Milton, "could wield / These Elements" (*PL* 6.221-22). When Wordsworth writes that the Spanish guerrillas "have learnt to open and to close / The ridges of grim war" (31.3-4), he expects us not only to recognize the Miltonic allusion but to recall the earlier poet's description in the same context of the democratic quality of the principles of guidance shown by Heaven's angelic heroic host. In Milton's language:

> Leader seem'd
> Each Warrior single as in Chief, expert
> When to advance, or stand, or turn the sway
> Of Battle, open when, and when to close
> The ridges of grim War; no thought of flight
> None of retreat, no unbecoming deed
> That argu'd fear; each on himself reli'd,
> As only in his arm the moment lay
> Of victory.
>
> (*PL* 6.232-40)

Such are the necessary guides of unerring skill in war as in peace, in politics and military enterprises as in poetry.

Among the nameless commonality of high-minded guides, spokesmen, and warriors, the noble Living of the Iberian struggle, are two exceptions, two *named* heroes. They are Palafox (mentioned in sonnets XXII and XXIII) and Mina (in sonnet XXXI). José Rebolledo Palafox y Melci was the hero who commanded the defense of Zaragoza at the time of the French siege of that city in 1808–09. But he was a peculiar example of a living hero at the time the sonnets were composed, for at the fall of Zaragoza in February 1809, Palafox was taken prisoner by the French, held incommunicado for five years in the castle at Vincennes, and presumed dead. "Ah! where is Palafox?" writes Wordsworth, "Nor tongue nor pen / Reports of him, his dwelling or his grave!" (23.1–2). But the poet seems to have feared the worst. Although expressing a hope that "once again / . . . we shall hail thee, Champion Brave," the sonnet points instead to an opposite conclusion: "Unbounded is the might / Of martyrdom" (23.5–6, 9–10). The insistent suggestion here and throughout the whole series of sonnets is that dead heroes make the safest guides, at least in military affairs.

The heroic Mina mentioned in sonnet XXXI is a similarly peculiar representative of the noble Living. The note in the de Selincourt-Darbishire edition of *Poetical Works* (3:460) which identifies him as "Don Esprez y Mina" (the accurate name is Francisco Espoz y Mina) appears to be in error. Wordsworth's Mina would be instead the nephew of General Espoz y Mina, a young man named Francisco Javier Mina, who, as a student at Zaragoza, helped organize other students there in the city's resistance to the French siege. (Wordsworth describes him appropriately as "Mina nourished in the studious shade"—

31.11.) This young Francisco Javier Mina became a popular and internationally known hero and guide, but he suffered the same temporary fate as Palafox: captured by the French, he too was held incommunicado in Vincennes castle until 1814. At the time of Wordsworth's writing, then, he too was missing and presumed dead. The poet compares him to "that great Leader," Sertorius, who had longed for burial after *his* death (31.12-14).

The only two living heroes identified by name in the Iberian sonnets were, then, believed to be dead at the time that Wordsworth writes of them. They belong, in the poet's plan, not among the noble Living but the noble Dead; they are intended as the most famous recent examples of dead guides. The distinction is important, indeed crucial, in understanding Wordsworth's views on what constitutes trustworthy guidance and just who can qualify as a trusted guide. In the *Cintra* tract, the poet had written, "There is an unconquerable tendency in all power, save that of knowledge acting by and through knowledge, to injure the mind of him who exercises that power; so much so that best natures cannot escape the evil of such alliance" (308). Let me emphasize the point: any guide exercising any power or influence other than the power of pure mind and truth is inevitably corrupted. As the Solitary also discovered, as noted previously, power inevitably corrupts; it unconquerably corrupts even conquering heroes. Only death can place the human hero and guide beyond this corrupting influence and make him a safe guide and exemplar for the living defenders and seekers of liberty. The only identifiable heroes with names attached to them in the Iberian sonnets are all safely dead and incorruptible—Sertorius, Viriathus, and, as Wordsworth supposed, Palafox and Mina. All living guides could only be nameless members of the democratic throng—"and, throughout

Spain," exults the poet, "(Thanks to high God) forests of such remain" (28.10–11).

On the other hand, those to whom so many in Wordsworth's time, as in ours, looked for political guidance, warriors and government leaders, fare badly in these sonnets. Of the politicians, Wordsworth writes:

> O'erweening statesmen have full long relied
> On fleets and armies, and external wealth:
> But from *within* proceeds a nation's health;
> Which shall not fail, though poor men cleave with
>   pride
> To the paternal floor.
>
> (29.1–5)

Proper guidance, we have repeatedly seen, requires unerring skill in the guide and unconquerable integrity in the guided. If "o'erweening Statesmen" rely, as sonnet XXIX says, on the unreliable, however, the truth about high-principled liberty is safe in democratic hands and hearts, safe with "Spaniards of every rank, by whom the good / Of such high course was felt and understood" (29.10–11).

Nor do warriors, especially British generals, gain entry to Wordsworth's hall of heroes and trustworthy guides. The qualities essential to combat the inevitable tendency of power to corrupt its possessors he finds to be extinct in both "the Political or Military Functionary" (*Cintra* 307). Military power, then, is really a kind of self-limiting weakness:

> The power of Armies is a visible thing,
> Formal and circumscribed in time and space;

But who the limits of that power shall trace
Which a brave People into light can bring
Or hide, at will,—for freedom combating.

(32.1-5)

The Iberian sonnets, even while denying the efficacy of military force as a reliable guide to freedom, continue to affirm Wordsworth's democratic belief expressed earlier in the *Cintra* tract that "the cause of the People . . . is safe while it remains not only in the bosom but in the hands of the People" (318). The irregular armies of the peoples of Iberia, the ubiquitous guerrillas, constantly dispersed, constantly reuniting "as a flight / Of scattered quails by signs do reunite" (30.6-7), never defeated though always "far outnumbered by their Foes" (31.2), these freedom fighters are the real living guides and heroes of the sonnets. Wordsworth celebrates their courage and resourcefulness, but above all he glories in their spiritual power. He observes that even while they stand with "sword . . . at the Foeman's heart" (30.12), their chief strength, and their main effect on Napoleon himself, is in their ability to "hang like dreams around his guilty bed" (30.14).

This remarkable sequence of sonnets, then, affords valuable and specific insights into Wordsworth's political idealism, his search for trustworthy guides for society, during a period when lost leaders and lost opportunities in the struggle against Napoleon might have discouraged him, as happened with some others, into seeking hope and solace in other principles and other kinds of guides. The kind of guides a great many people look to, especially in troubled times, for political leadership remained for Wordsworth, even in this Iberian crisis, unthinkable:

Never may from our souls one truth depart—
That an accursed thing it is to gaze
On prosperous tyrants with a dazzled eye.
(33.7–9)

We see then that Wordsworth's interest in principles of guidance, in the requirements of a trustworthy guide and, equally, in the retention of independence and integrity by the guided, was a lifelong concern which involved him in very frequent musings on major issues of politics and poetics, on education and epistemological theory. Almost all guides, especially human guides, proved fallible in the poet's considerations.

Where, then, is trust to be placed? The question calls to mind the judgment on Wordsworth offered by Ralph Waldo Emerson on the occasion of his visit to Wordsworth at Rydal Mount almost at the end of the poet's life, in March 1848. Writes Emerson: "Let us say of him that, alone in his time, he treated the human mind well, and with an absolute trust" (1930). This is high and well-deserved praise. But even better is Wordsworth's own statement, those lines in *Prelude* 10 where he speaks of the individual human mind and spirit being thoroughly true to its own nature and thereby qualifying to serve as the final, the trusted guide:

A spirit strong
In hope, and trained to noble aspirations,
A spirit thoroughly faithful to itself,
Is for Society's unreasoning herd
A domineering instinct, serves at once
For way and guide, a fluent receptacle

That gathers up each petty straggling rill
And vein of water, glad to be rolled on
In safe obedience; . . . a mind, whose rest
Is where it ought to be, in self-restraint,
In circumspection and simplicity,
Falls rarely in entire discomfiture
Below its aim, or meets with, from without,
A treachery that foils it or defeats;
And, lastly, if the means on human will,
Frail human will, dependent should betray
Him who too boldly trusted them, I felt
That 'mid the loud distractions of the world
A sovereign voice subsists within the soul,
Arbiter undisturbed of right and wrong,
Of life and death, in majesty severe
Enjoining, as may best promote the aims
Of truth and justice, either sacrifice,
From whatsoever region of our cares
Or our infirm affections nature pleads,
Earnest and blind, against the stern decree.

(165–90)

Here, then, to this conclusion, the poet guides us from his lifelong ardent meditations on principles of leadership and teaching. Here is the pinnacle of his truth, beyond political theories and theorists, beyond even the noblest books, beyond the rivers and clouds and guiding light of external nature, even beyond Urania, beyond the great God himself—trust in the "greater Muse" Wordsworth had hoped for. It is a lofty objective, and its pursuit is rigorous and unending in its demands; but Wordsworth's discovery of the ultimately reliable principle of trust and leading provides for the poet, and for us his students, the one indisputable "way and guide." It is within the ability of all human beings, search though they will for less reliable guides and schemes of guidance. It is not social but individual, for "the destiny of Man . . . still / [Hangs] upon single persons" (10.155–56). It is, simply, powerfully, inescapably, the indwelling divinity of guidance, the "sovereign voice," found in every human "spirit thoroughly faithful to itself."

WORKS CITED

Abrams, Meyer H., ed. *English Romantic Poets: Modern Essays in Criticism.* 2nd ed. Oxford: Oxford UP, 1975.

Auden, W. H. Introduction. *Selected Poetry and Prose of Byron.* Ed. Auden. New York: New American Library, 1966. vii–xxiv.

"Babes in the Woods." *R. Caldecott's Picture Book.* No. 1. London: Frederick Warne, n.d.

Bateson, F. W. *Wordsworth: A Re-interpretation.* London: Longmans, 1956.

Baugh, Albert C., ed. *A Literary History of England.* 2nd ed. New York: Appleton, 1967.

Blake, William. *The Complete Poetry and Prose of William Blake.* Ed. David V. Erdman. Berkeley: U of California P, 1982.

Burney, Charles. Rev. of *Lyrical Ballads,* by Wordsworth and Coleridge. *Monthly Review* 2nd ser. 29 (June 1799): 202–10.

Byron, George Gordon (Lord). *Byron's Letters and Journals.* Ed. Leslie A. Marchand. 12 vols. London: John Murray, 1973–82.

———. *Don Juan.* Ed. Jerome J. McGann. Oxford: Clarendon, 1986. Vol. 5 of *Lord Byron: The Complete Poetical Works.* 1980–. 5 vols. to date.

———. Rev. of *Poems,* by Wordsworth. 2 vols. *Monthly Literary Recreations* 3 (July 1807): 65–66.

Coleridge, Samuel Taylor. *Biographia Literaria.* Ed. John Shawcross. 2 vols. Oxford: Clarendon, 1907.

Coleridge, Samuel Taylor (*continued*)

———. *Biographia Literaria*. Ed. George Watson. London: Dent, 1965.

———. *Collected Letters*. Ed. Earl Leslie Griggs. 6 vols. Oxford: Clarendon, 1956–71.

———. *Selected Poems*. Ed. R. C. Bald. New York: Appleton, 1956.

Collier, John Payne. Rev. of *The Poetic Mirror, or the Living Bards of Britain*, by James Hogg. *Critical Review* 4 (Nov. 1816): 466–67.

Colville, Derek. *The Teaching of Wordsworth*. New York: Peter Lang, 1984.

Crabbe, George. *The Poetical Works of George Crabbe*. London: Routledge, 1858.

Daube, David. *The Sudden in the Scriptures*. Leiden: Brill, 1964.

De Quincey, Thomas. *The Collected Writings of Thomas De Quincey*. Ed. David Masson. 14 vols. New York: AMS, 1968.

———. Letter to Wordsworth, 31 May 1803, in *Recollections of the Lakes and the Lake Poets*. Ed. David Wright. Baltimore: Penguin, 1970.

Dibdin, Thomas. *Library Companion, or the Young Man's Guide and the Old Man's Comfort in the Choice of a Library*. London, 1824.

Elwin, Malcolm. *The First Romantics*. New York: Longmans, 1948.

Emerson, Ralph Waldo. *English Traits*. Ed. Howard Mumford Jones. Cambridge: Belnap/Harvard UP, 1966.

Fruman, Norman. *Coleridge, the Damaged Archangel*. New York: Braziller, 1971.

George, Andrew J., ed. *The Complete Poetical Works of Wordsworth*. Boston: Houghton, 1932.

Hartman, Geoffrey H. *Wordsworth's Poetry, 1787–1814*. New Haven: Yale UP, 1971.

Havens, Raymond Dexter. "Simplicity, a Changing Concept." *JEGP* 14 (1953): 28–36.

Hazlitt, William. *The Complete Works of William Hazlitt*. Ed. P. P. Howe. 21 vols. New York: AMS, 1967.

Hobhouse, John Cam (Lord Broughton). *Recollections of a Long Life*. Ed. Lady Dorchester. 2 vols. New York: AMS, 1968.

Hollander, John. *The Figure of Echo: A Mode of Allusion in Milton and After*. Berkeley: U of California P, 1981.

Hopkins, Gerard Manley. *Poems of Gerard Manley Hopkins*. Ed. Robert Bridges. 3rd ed. rev. W. H. Gardner. New York: Oxford UP, 1948.

"Instruction." *OED*. Compact ed., 1971.

Jacobus, Mary. *Tradition and Experiment in Wordsworth's* Lyrical Ballads *(1798)*. Oxford: Oxford UP, 1976.

Jeffrey, Francis. Rev. of *Poems*, by Wordsworth. *Edinburgh Review* 11 (Oct. 1807): 214–31.

_____. Rev. of current publications. *Edinburgh Review* 12 (Apr. 1808): 137–40.

Jordan, John E. "The Novelty of the *Lyrical Ballads*." *Bicentenary Wordsworth Studies in Memory of John Alban Finch*. Ed. Jonathan Wordsworth. Ithaca: Cornell UP, 1970. 340–58.

_____. *Why the* Lyrical Ballads? Berkeley: U of California P, 1976.

Kroeber, Karl. *Romantic Narrative Art*. Madison: U of Wisconsin P, 1966.

Langbaum, Robert. *The Poetry of Experience*. New York: Random, 1957.

Lehman, B. H. *Carlyle's Theory of the Hero: Its Sources, Development, History, and Influence on Carlyle's Work*. Durham: Duke UP, 1928.

_____. "The Doctrine of Leadership in the Greater Romantic Poets." *PMLA* 37 (1922): 639–61.

Mant, Richard. *The Simpliciad; a Satirico-didactic Poem . . . .* London, 1808.

Milton, John. *John Milton: Complete Poems and Major Prose.* Ed. Merritt Y. Hughes. New York: Odyssey, 1957.

Parrish, Stephen. " 'The Thorn': Wordsworth's Dramatic Monologue." *ELH* 27 (1957): 153-63.

Pope, Alexander. *The Twickenham Edition of the Poems of Alexander Pope.* Gen. ed. John Butt. 11 vols. London: Methuen, 1950-59.

Reed, Mark. *Wordsworth: The Chronology of the Middle Years.* Cambridge: Harvard UP, 1975.

Ryskamp, Charles. "Wordsworth's *Lyrical Ballads* in Their Time." *From Sensibility to Romanticism: Essays Presented to Frederick A. Pottle.* Ed. F. W. Hilles and Harold Bloom. New York: Oxford UP, 1965. 357-72.

Scholes, Robert. "Language, Narrative, and Anti-Narrative." *Critical Inquiry* 7 (1980): 204-12.

Shakespeare, William. *The Riverside Shakespeare.* Ed. G. Blakemore Evans. Boston: Houghton, 1974.

Shelley, Percy Bysshe. *Prometheus Unbound. Shelley's Poetry and Prose.* Ed. Donald H. Reiman and Sharon B. Powers. New York: Norton, 1977. 130-210.

Smith, Elsie. *An Estimate of William Wordsworth by His Contemporaries.* Oxford: Oxford UP, 1932.

Southey, Robert. Rev. of *Lyrical Ballads,* by Wordsworth and Coleridge. *Critical Review* (Oct. 1798): 197-204.

Spenser, Edmund. *The Poems of Spenser.* Ed. J. C. Smith and Ernest de Selincourt. London: Oxford UP, 1912.

Steffan, Truman G., and Willis W. Pratt, eds. *Don Juan: Variorum Edition.* 4 vols. Austin: U of Texas P, 1957.

"Teacher." *OED.* Compact ed., 1971.

Walpole, Horace. *Horace Walpole's Correspondence with Sir Horace Mann.* Ed. W. S. Lewis, Warren Hunting Smith, and George L. Lam. 4 vols. New Haven: Yale UP, 1960.

Ward, A. W., and G. P. Gooch, eds. *The Cambridge History of British Foreign Policy*. 3 vols. New York: Macmillan, 1922–23.

Warton, Joseph. *Essay on the Writings and Genius of Pope*. London, 1756.

Woodring, Carl. *Politics in English Romantic Poetry*. Cambridge: Harvard UP, 1970.

_____, ed. *Prose of the Romantic Period*. Boston: Houghton, 1961.

Woolf, Virginia. *A Writer's Diary*. Ed. Leonard Woolf. New York: Harcourt, 1954.

Wordsworth, Dorothy. *Journals of Dorothy Wordsworth*. Ed. Mary Moorman. London: Oxford UP, 1973.

Wordsworth, William. *The Poetical Works of William Wordsworth*. 1940–49. Ed. Ernest de Selincourt and Helen Darbishire. 5 vols. Oxford: Clarendon, 1952–59.

_____. *The Prelude, or Growth of a Poet's Mind*. Ed. Ernest de Selincourt, rev. Helen Darbishire. Oxford: Clarendon, 1959.

_____. *The Prelude, or Growth of a Poet's Mind*. Ed. Ernest de Selincourt. Rev. Helen Darbishire. Oxford: Clarendon, 1959.

Wordsworth, William, and Dorothy Wordsworth. *The Letters of William and Dorothy Wordsworth*. Vol. 1, *The Early Years*. Ed. Chester L. Shaver. Vols. 2 and 3, *The Middle Years*. Ed. Mary Moorman and Alan G. Hill. Vol. 4–6 to date, *The Later Years*. Ed. Alan G. Hill. Oxford: Clarendon, 1967–. 6 vols. to date.

Wordsworth, William, and Mary Wordsworth. *The Love Letters of William and Mary Wordsworth*. Ed. Beth Darlington. London: Chatto, 1982.

Wordsworth, William, and Samuel Taylor Coleridge. *Lyrical Ballads, 1798*. Ed. W. J. B. Owen. 2nd ed. London: Oxford UP, 1969.

INDEX

DATE DUE

GAYLORD			PRINTED IN U.S.A.